# OHPIKIIHAAKAN-OHPIHMEH

## RAISED SOMEWHERE ELSE

# OHPIKIIHAAKAN-OHPIHMEH

## RAISED SOMEWHERE ELSE

A 60s Scoop Adoptee's Story of Coming Home

Colleen Cardinal

Foreword by Raven Sinclair

**Roseway Publishing**
an imprint of Fernwood Publishing
Halifax & Winnipeg

Editing: Raven Sinclair and Jane Butler
Cover image: *Blessings* by Christopher Rowland
Design: Tania Craan
Printed and bound in Canada

Published by Roseway Publishing
an imprint of Fernwood Publishing
32 Oceanvista Lane, Black Point, Nova Scotia, B0J 1B0
and 748 Broadway Avenue, Winnipeg, Manitoba, R3G 0x3
www.fernwoodpublishing.ca/roseway

Fernwood Publishing Company Limited gratefully acknowledges the financial
support of the Government of Canada, the Canada Council for the Arts, the
Province of Manitoba, the Province of Nova Scotia and Arts Nova Scotia.

Library and Archives Canada Cataloguing in Publication

Cardinal, Colleen, author
Ohpikiihaakan-ohpihmeh = Raised somewhere else: a 60s Scoop
adoptee's story of coming home / Colleen Cardinal.

Issued in print and electronic formats.
ISBN 978-1-77363-020-5 (softcover).—ISBN 978-1-77363-021-2 (EPUB).—
ISBN 978-1-77363-022-9 (Kindle)

1. Cardinal, Colleen. 2. Adopted children—Canada—Biography.
3. Autobiographies. I. Title. II. Title: Raised somewhere else.

HV874.82.C37A3 2018        306.874092        C2017-907871-2
                    C2017-907872-0

# Kiskisonaw kahkiiyaw ka-saakihaayaakik

# We Remember All Our Loved Ones

THIS BOOK IS DEDICATED to all our Indigenous relations. It is for those who are missing or murdered, homeless, incarcerated, living and struggling with addiction, chronic pain, disease, poverty, and mental illness. It is for those experiencing and surviving systemic racism through media and policies meant to dehumanize, eradicate and erase our identity, our sovereignty and our ceremonies that connect us to the land our ancestors have lived on since time immemorial.

I honour my blood relatives, all of whom have been impacted by violent colonial policies created by the Canadian government, which separated, destroyed and traumatized our family and which still wreak havoc upon Indigenous children and families.

I dedicate this book to my late eldest sister, Eugenia (Gina) Charmaine Desa; my late mother Dolly Esther Cardinal née Cryer; my late *kokum* Maggie Cryer; my maternal aunties June Cryer, Cecelia Cryer, Helen Cryer, Roseanne Cryer and Albertine Cryer; my maternal uncle Marvin Cryer; my paternal uncles Dennis, Bruce and Fred; my Aunt Yvonne; my late *kokum* Helen Jackson-Brettron; my nephew Stephen Allen Sawyer; and lastly my sister-in-law Lynn Minia Jackson, paternal aunty to my sons.

Gina, Dakota, Colleen

# Foreword

## by Raven Sinclair

THE SIXTIES SCOOP IS a term that refers to the Indigenous child removal system in Canada that spans the late 1950s to the present day. Thousands of Indigenous children were adopted into white settler Canadian families, with most of those adoptions taking place in the 1960s and 1970s. Children were apprehended in large numbers. Some First Nations communities lost virtually all their children in certain age groups. Children were adopted and fostered into families of all sorts, and according to Justice Edwin Kimelman and Bridget Moran, a British Columbia social worker in the 1960s, homes were often not adequately assessed for suitability or safety. Some children were fortunate to find loving families, while many thousands of others suffered all forms of abuse and neglect as well as racism from within their adoptive family units. Bridget Moran (1992) stated that the "BC child welfare system was the biggest contributor to child abuse in the province."

Colleen's story is one among tens of thousands. What makes her story unique is that she has found the inner strength to write it down and share it with others. Her honesty in telling about the abuses and obstacles that confronted her at almost every step of her journey is evident on every page. Her story will draw you in immediately and you may find it difficult to put the book down because you begin to wonder what can possibly happen next. Her story does not sensationalize her experiences, even the horrific ones. She writes in a matter-of-fact way and the reader becomes a witness on the journey of her life to the present. The ride is occasionally frightening and sad, which makes the funny moments a welcome relief. As a witness, we get to understand how strength and courage can result from trauma, and we breathe a sigh of relief with Colleen as she emerges from some very dark times. We also get to see, with some awe, that she has become a shining light in her own right: a social justice advocate, community organizer extraordinaire, and a compassionate and loving mom and loyal friend.

While none of this justifies what Colleen had to go through, it does inspire us to re-evaluate the Indigenous child removal system in Canada. It also inspires our admiration for Colleen and the many others with similar experiences who not only survived but thrived in ways that show the incredible resilience and tenacity of the human spirit.

# Tapeyihtamiwin

# Reckoning

THE ONLY THING I'VE known about myself for the past twenty-eight years is that I am completely and utterly devoted to my children. I believe they saved my life. They kept me going when I so often wanted to give up. I would drag myself out of bed on countless mornings and have hope that things would change and get better one day. Everything I have done up until this point was to provide a better life for my children: my sobriety, leaving abusive relationships and going back to school so I could escape poverty and get off Ontario Works. I began having children when I was sixteen years old and still a child myself. I did not plan on having children but I am grateful for them every single day because their spirits chose me to be their mother.

This is my story of how I came to know who I am as *nēhiiyēw iskew*, adopted and raised in a non-Indigenous household thousands of kilometres away from my territory. When I started to unravel my past and find out where I came from, it led to critical life changes and eventually to healing, but most importantly, it has led to peace and understanding.

I am not perfect by any means and have hurt and been violent to other people in my past. I have also been hurt and had extreme physical, sexual and emotional violence committed against me throughout my life. I have yelled, raged, screamed at the top of my lungs, thrown things, sworn at people, made racist and homophobic slurs, hated and wished horrible things for people who have hurt me. I have been jealous, irrational, emotional, selfish and even vain. I have also loved deeply, tenderly held my newborn babies, cried when my grandbabies were born, forgiven those who hurt me and inflicted abuse on me, cried and wept until my belly went into muscle spasms from the pain of grief. I have reconciled my pain with most of my abusers, walked away from toxic relationships, learned to love and respect myself, and finally, to extend the tenderness my children needed from me so badly.

In 1989 I reconnected with my biological family in Edmonton, Alberta. It was a bittersweet experience. I lived through a lot of physical and sexual violence in my life and it was only after I moved back to Sault Ste. Marie in 1998 that I began my healing journey, rediscovering my culture though prayer, sweat lodges and ceremonies. I write and tell my story from my point of view, but also to honour my sisters' stories and to validate the experiences of hundreds of other Indigenous adoptees and foster care survivors of the 60s Scoop. You are not alone, sisters and brothers.

For years I believed I did not have the right to speak out, to complain or to acknowledge that my childhood was traumatic. My adulthood is a murky mess from all the dysfunction I've experienced. Not knowing where you belong in society or having a group or family to identify with is very lonely.

This story is about growing up in an adoptive home with a non-Indigenous brother and parents. It is about the rules set out in the household that segregated my sisters and me and ensured we were treated far differently from their biological son. My sisters and I suffered tremendous abuse — physical, emotional, sexual and spiritual abuse — and it impacted our lives as young adults and now as adults with children.

4

It has only been in the last five years that I have realized the degree of damage caused by the 60s Scoop of Indigenous children across Canada. I knew that my sisters and I had been through something traumatizing that changed our lives, but I see now that it had lasting effects that my remaining sister and I cope with today.[1]

The 60s Scoop was an aggressive tool for assimilation and cultural genocide through the Canadian child welfare system. Now, I have had people say to me, "Your life turned out better because you were raised in an adoptive home by white people," but I beg to differ. Sure, I had opportunities like sports and travel, but by and large I was robbed of a life that I will never get back. My biological parents were both fluent Cree speakers, and I had a very large extended family of aunts, uncles and cousins all over Saddle Lake/Goodfish Lake and the surrounding area that I cannot re-integrate into. I lost the protection, familiarity and socialization opportunities of knowing my own people, and by "people" I mean Nehiyawak (Plains Cree) within my own territory. That *cannot* be replaced. I grew up feeling homesick and unsettled in the adoptive household, ready to run away at any sign of danger.

Recently, I watched a program called *The 8th Fire* on CBC, where, in a discussion of the 60s Scoop, a woman who had been adopted spoke of being picked from a catalogue of Indigenous children. I was shocked to hear this because my mother told me that my sisters and I had been picked out of a catalogue. In my mind I keep wondering how this came about; who did the gathering and collecting of photos and files of Indigenous children? The federal government was harvesting Indigenous children to be farmed out to good "white" homes in a way very similar

---

1. There are a lot of resources available but one that I found useful is "Implications of the Sixties Scoop" <http://www1.uwindsor.ca/criticalsocialwork/the-sixties-scoop-implications-for-social-workers-and-social-work-education>.

Memorandum of agreement respecting
welfare programs for Indians
between the Government of Canada
and the Government of the Province of Ontario

**1966**

Memorandum of Agreement between Ontario and Canada

to the Residential Schools initiative to "take the Indian out of the child." Many Canadians to this day have no idea about it. Indigenous children were systematically and deliberately put into white, European homes to be assimilated.

In 2009, I heard about a few class action lawsuits being launched against the Canadian government for contributing to cultural genocide of thousands of First Nations children. The Brown and Commanda legal proceeding against the government is one that I applied to. A friend of mine sent me a link to the website and a contact email, suggesting that I take part as a class member. Jeffrey Wilson of Wilson Christen law firm had released a document regarding Indigenous adoptees interested in a class action lawsuit. The claim refers to a Canada–Ontario Welfare Agreement that allowed for the removal and placement of Indigenous children into non-Indigenous families, thus systematically denying their inherent right to language, culture and First Nations identity.

These were the guidelines stipulated in the documents for the plaintiffs to qualify:

This is a case about loss of culture of First Nations persons, status and non-status Indigenous persons in the sense that claimants were denied or had taken from them knowledge of their biological parents, siblings, extended family, their birth names, their spiritual connections, their language, their customs, and their genealogy. The plaintiffs are claiming "breach of fiduciary duty" and "negligence" on the part of the defendant, the Federal Government of Canada.

Claimants in the lawsuit are limited to:

(A) People who are First Nations (including status, non-status, Metis,

(B) Those who were placed in a non-First Nations environment

(C) Those who experienced their loss/denial in Ontario

(D) Those who experienced their loss/denial between January 1, 1965 and December 31, 1984.
‹http://www.sixtiesscoopclaim.ca/›

Given that my adoption had been finalized in Ontario and my loss and denial had taken place in Ontario, I applied to be a part of the Brown and Commanda lawsuit.

At the time I realized I had barely scraped the surface of the pain, anger and suffering I had refused to allow myself to feel all these years. I could never put my finger on exactly what it was that was missing from my life but I knew something very wrong had happened to my sisters and me. Finding out hundreds or possibly thousands of other children had been through the same experience validated me. I remember reading the document for the first time, trying to read it to my kids who hadn't a clue what I was referring to. I couldn't sleep, eat or sit still; learning that there were other people just like me had exhilarated and motivated me to find out more. That high lasted a few days before reality set in and memories flowed back. The announcement of this class action lawsuit set me off into crisis mode once again.

~~~

Rarely have I felt stable and at peace emotionally but at this

(1) In this agreement, unless otherwise specified,

(a) "Aggregate Ontario Welfare Program" means the aggregate of all provincial welfare programs available to the general population of the province;

(b) "Indian" means a person who, pursuant to the Indian Act, is registered as an Indian, or is entitled to be registered as an Indian;

(c) "Indians with Reserve Status" means (except where otherwise designated by Canada and Ontario by agreement) Indians who are

(i) resident on an Indian reserve;

(ii) resident on Crown land, or in territory without municipal organization in the Province, or

(iii) designated as such by the Minister of Northern Affairs and National Resources;

(d) "the Province" means the Province of Ontario;

(e) "Provincial Welfare Program" means a welfare program (whether privately, municipally or provincially operated) to which public money of the Province is or may be contributed, applicable or available generally to residents of the Province and, without restricting the generality of the

Agreement

point in my life, I feel alive. I am no longer just surviving. There are no more crisis modes or triggers that make me want to run. I guess it is that time in my life when I am at a crossroads, trying to understand who I am, what events have shaped me into the person I am today, and perhaps trying to find some peace from writing my story and sharing it with others who may have been through similar experiences. My children may read this one day; if so, I hope they can understand and forgive me for being the overbearing, emotional mess of a mother I was. I want them to know that I did my best and what I thought was right. My overprotectiveness may have seemed unfair to them, but in all honesty I only wanted the best for them and to protect them from the hurts I experienced as a child.

Like a familiar piece of luggage, I have dragged my abuse right along with me, and in many ways have taken it out on my children. I believe the physical, emotional and sexual abuse I experienced manifests itself physically and sits in my stomach, where the fat overhangs my jeans and pushes against the buttons that leave their imprint on my midsection. I believe the abuse leaks out of my pores and onto my skin as psoriasis so everyone can see my damaged soul and how my body has betrayed me. The Bell's Palsy is a reminder of my vanity and how the ugliness of it was reflected in my soul. It is a constant reminder of how I treated people based on their looks, and it tells me I have to do better every single day.

My immune system has been pushed to the edge by constant anxiety and hyper-vigilance, by trying to control each and every situation, scanning for danger, watching for warning signs and any potential threats to my children and me.

It is exhausting to live on the edge, waiting for the worst thing to happen, and my greatest fear was of not being prepared when it did. I know now that I am ready to share: all the shame, guilt, trauma, pain, and also my joys, successes, happiness and inspiration.

I used to get bored as a child. Even now as an adult, I get bored if I am not constantly stimulated, which sometimes leads to trouble. I used to complain about being bored and my adoptive mother used to say, "You can't have fun all the time, Colleen." I despised this comment and remember saying, "Why not? Why can't I have fun all the time?" Even as an adult I felt like I should be having fun all the time and took nothing seriously. I shrugged off everything or detached from life. My goal was to have unrestricted fun at any cost and deal with the consequences later. The problem was, I never did deal with the consequences later; they just piled up. The fun started to run out when the memories came back, and everything came to a head when my past caught up with me. I cannot run anymore. There is nowhere left to go. I've been making the same old mistakes because my past haunts me, it holds on like a jagged nail caught on my sweater. It grates on my nerves, irritates me, and turns to acid in my stomach. Squeezing my eyes shut to block out memory isn't as effective as it once was. I cannot stop the memories and sequester them or let my body absorb them any more. What do I do? It's time to confront it all.

This book has taken over five years to write. When the first draft was done, I wanted to burn it. I never intended to publish it but I mentioned it to Raven and she insisted upon reading it. She said she couldn't put it down and then pestered me (in a good way) to publish it. She said every adoptee has a story to tell and it is time to get our stories out there. Me, I just wanted to get the memories onto paper and out of my head. When it was done, I felt like I had vomited a lifetime into these pages. At first, writing about the abuse and all the bad things came out easy; it was harder to write about the good stuff and the healing journey. That piece took longer to develop, years in fact.

Writing has been healing for me even though it required painstaking emotional accounts of terrible shame, sadness, hurt, humiliation, loneliness, grief and anger. It has been like the waves of the Atlantic Ocean crashing on me, shocking me with icy cold awareness and then painfully dragging my raw body across the sand, ripping my skin and tearing at my soul. My story is a million tiny tears being shed so you can see the anguish, the survival and the love.

# CHAPTER 1

## E-maskamih cik

MY STORY BEGINS WITH my biological mother, Dolly Esther Cardinal, née Cryer, born September 5, 1950. She was one of fifteen children, and my *kokum*'s name was Maggie Cryer. Esther was registered to Treaty Six territory, Onihcikiskowapowin (Saddle Lake Cree Nation), in Alberta. She attended Blue Quills Residential School from 1962–1966, until she was sixteen. It was only in 2013 while writing this book that I discovered this information. There is no record or even an oral history account of Esther's whereabouts after she left residential school. No stories have been shared with me as to what happened and why she ended up in Edmonton. Somewhere along that journey she met my father, Richard Paul Cardinal, who was also from Onihcikiskowapowin First Nation. Some stories were shared that they married just before I was born, but nevertheless they had three children: my oldest sister Gina, born in 1970, my middle sister Dakota, born in 1971, and me, Colleen, born in 1972.

My adoption records show I was a wee baby when I was taken from my parents in the first year of my life. I've been told a few stories about when we were young: sleeping in a dresser drawer as an infant, being dropped by one of my mom's sisters,

Dolly Esther Cardinal, née Cryer

and also being called by the nickname "baby."

My father Ricky stated that there were many parties in the home and I was neglected and put in harm's way at these parties. Esther claimed Ricky used to beat her severely and was an abusive man. My father claims that my mother's family used to pile up on him and beat him up; I believe the truth is somewhere in the middle. Maybe he did beat her, and in retaliation her family beat him up too. I can totally believe that, as dysfunctional as it sounds. Anything was possible. Ricky told me different stories now and then; he portrayed himself as a dangerous bad boy who used to shoot up whiskey in his arms, fight anyone who got in his way and stick up for himself against people who disrespected him. He told me a tale of robbing a bank and hiding the money in an alleyway in the rafters of a garage. In Edmonton there are back alleys to a lot of the streets, with garages lining them. He explained that he was being chased so he hid the money in the rafters, and when he went back for it later he couldn't remember which garage rafter he had left it in. I laughed and encouraged him to try and find it so we could cash in on his bank robbing,. I wanted so badly to believe him.

My father Ricky has maintained, over the years since I reconnected with him in 1989, that my sisters and I were given to child welfare by my mom, yet paperwork demonstrates we were taken due to "neglect, unfit conditions, and severe alcohol issues."

Ricky also maintains he was working the night shift when we were taken, that Esther had a big party and in the morning when he got home, her brothers and sisters ganged up on him, beat him senseless and he ended up in the hospital. This is where the story gets muddled because neither one of my parents were clear about what actually took place or when the "taking" of us girls happened. Ricky claims it happened while he was in the hospital, that upon release he came home to find us girls gone

Richard Paul Cardinal

for good, and as my mom told him, we were given to a nice couple who owned a farm in Calgary. My father insists that he looked for us but just gave up after a while. Esther never offered her version of what happened after we were taken.

My eldest sister Gina was born on February 2, 1970, and she was called Wesakacihp (Little Groundhog) because it was Groundhog Day. She was feisty, outgoing and a very funny young girl. I remember her being silly at times and also being a leader, unafraid to stand up for her little sisters or even to stand up to our adoptive father, Ronald.[1] Gina loved dogs and would lavish attention on our family pets. She was my hero and at times the villain in my life because she would also restrain me by sitting on me and tickling me until I cried. Gina was slim with long curly hair, crooked front teeth, faint freckles and she always smelled like fresh air in the fall — always.

Dakota was born on April 27, 1971, and I remember her as shy, with pretty features and an awkwardness that made her seem more vulnerable. Dakota was a beauty, with a heart-shaped

---

1 Pseudonyms have been used.

face, a sweet smile and a willingness to go along with the crowd. She was a follower and boy-crazy in her teenage years. I always remember Dakota being the one who was most damaged by living in the White home. She was mercilessly picked on by my adoptive brother Scott and his father, who continually referred to her as a "fat, ugly squaw," and at that time there was no talking back to our father or brother. At the supper table she sat to Ronald's right and across from Scott, at their mercy. I know Scott would kick her under the table and not get in trouble for it; she was the inevitable victim of these ongoing abusive behaviours.

We were in a few unsavoury foster homes between the years 1972 and 1975. I can recall being pushed around in a baby bathtub by my sisters, sitting at the top of the stairs with my sisters listening to drinking parties and people fighting, and one terrible instance when Dakota drank nail polish and was rushed to the hospital. These memories are patchy but I do recall these places *not* being our home.

In 1975 my sisters and I were placed together in a non-Indigenous household in Sault Ste. Marie, Ontario. The White household was 3,000 kilometres away from our Treaty Six Territory but we had no concept of how far from our birth parents we were. I remember the journey as a plane ride, a long car ride and finally being in a country setting in the middle of the night. I do not remember meeting my new white parents, Ronald and Mary White, and their biological son, Scott. My only memory is seeing the shadow outlines of them standing in the doorway with the light behind them — no faces. I have no memory of our adoption process; all I remember is that some nice ladies took us for a plane ride and left us behind with these strangers. I remember wishing they would come back — those ladies were tender and kind. I have no recollection of the days that followed the adoption; we just stayed there and this was where we lived. One day we called them "mom" and "dad," I suppose.

My sisters and I shared a bedroom. Dakota got the top bunk, I got the bottom and Gina had her own single bed. We shared a room right up until we ran away from home, one after the other, in our teens. I can remember things about my mom that were fun, like doing crafts; going skiing, skating and swimming; and being completely involved in every sport or activity that she found for us to do. Mary literally filled up each moment of our lives with piano lessons, sports, crafts, chores, and if that wasn't enough, macramé and knitting. She also arranged for us to deliver flyers, newspapers, phonebooks and Sears catalogues. All of these earnings contributed to our upkeep in a family that treated us as second-class citizens. Of course at my tender age I had little understanding that I was being treated differently from Scott, the Whites' natural son.

I don't know when hyper-vigilance set in or if I was born with it and just learned how to refine it, but I remember being aware of my surroundings at a very young age. I remember watching and waiting for signs of danger. I was aware of tone of voice; I listened for footfalls and paid attention to the way a drawer or door was shut. If it was hard and forceful I knew my dad was angry, and these were warning signs to stay out of the way. I also learned at a young age that my mother could not offer protection or comfort when he was in a bad mood. It was every girl for herself in that house. If I could have shrunk into a wall, I would have but instead I watched, listened and learned how to be invisible. How many children dread the weekend and going home after school? I grew to hate weekends and holidays because they meant inescapable, unknown terror. Did other children in my class feel this way too?

We lived approximately twenty-five kilometres from Sault Ste. Marie, Ontario, set back into the woods on a rural road about one and a half kilometres from the paved highway. The road leading to my childhood home was lined with deciduous trees, mostly maple, birch and poplar. I can't deny that it was beautiful, so picturesque and wonderful on fall days to run down the road, swishing the leaves with our feet. The road was oiled every summer to keep the dust down, and my sisters and I would run on it road barefoot, not caring how black our feet got or that we might slip on the oil. Our feet were so tough and calloused that we felt no pain, and wearing shoes was a hindrance. Wearing shoes slowed you down and I would always end up forgetting them while I went on a new adventure with my sisters and friends.

The White residence was an old mobile trailer that was first used as a camp for the sawmill workers and later transformed into a double-wide trailer with an addition of two bedrooms. Eventually we added an upstairs with a garage. As a child I didn't know how lucky I was to grow up on a lakeside property with access to cool, clean water any time I pleased. I could canoe, fish and play in the water whenever I wanted. Ronald had landscaped the waterfront with walk-in cement steps and a sandy bottom. As far as I knew, our lakefront property was the only one with a sandy bottom, so we could walk out from knee to shoulder depth without having to touch the murky goo.

My sisters and I began swimming at a very young age and were competing alongside teenagers because our skills were that good. We could dive down to thirty metres and we'd make diving games with a diving bell and brick my adoptive father had fashioned. Ronald would throw it out as far as he could and we would compete to see who could get it first. The bell would shine deep in the bottom and after two or three tries we were always successful. Thirty metres is a long way to dive when you are eight and nine years old.

At the end of June, when the weather warmed up, we would race home from school and jump into the lake; the first swim was always the coldest! I grew up on the water and my best memories of my childhood were spent in the water, under the water, or floating on the water, staring up at the clouds or watching the patterns of the clouds on the hills across the lake.

Gina was by far the most daring and amazing of all of us girls. She was a leader blazing her way through, making friends and sometimes enemies as she went along. Sometimes her directness and daring ways rubbed people the wrong way and she would need to stand up for herself, but she was fearless — especially when it came to protecting her younger sisters. I worshipped my eldest sister and also feared her because I knew if I pissed her off or got on her nerves she would tickle me until I cried or punch me in the arm. She was the first to blaze the trail by running away and she attempted it twice; both times she was returned home and punished. She would tell me stories and I accepted them without a doubt because she would spin them in a way that made them believable. It was part of her charm. Gina would tell us tall tales about our birth parents, that they really wanted us and were fabulously rich and beautiful. She would tell Dakota and me tales of escaping, running away and how she would take care of us. I believed her and never doubted she would. Gina changed her name to Charmaine when she turned eighteen. I still think of her as Gina but sometimes I'll slip up and refer to her as Charmaine also.

My second-eldest sister, Dakota, was a quiet, nervous, awkward girl who either seemed to be forgotten about entirely or given the blame when something went wrong. Dakota had the most radiant smile of all of us girls and perfect teeth. My relationship with Dakota was never close. I don't remember very much about us playing together or about a significant time in our lives, but she was my sister and we lived through some very traumatic times together. Out of all of us girls, I think Dakota suffered the most.

I always wondered what our neighbours and family members thought about a white family adopting three Indigenous girls. Did they pity us or did we disgust them? I've tried to imagine the conversation where Ronald and Mary White announced to their family and friends, "We are adopting three Native girls from Alberta." Were they happy for my adoptive parents or did they wonder why this family would take three Indigenous children when they obviously could have children of their own? Did Mary have a baby shower — or in our case a "three little Indian" child adoption party? Were they happy to get three Indigenous kids or were we adopted out of pity?

Riding my bike up and down the road and pretending I was Ponch, from the early 80s TV show *CHiPs*, was my favourite form of escapism. My adoptive father had refurbished a second-hand bike for me and painted it black. There was nothing spectacular about it. In fact it was plain old ugly because you could tell it had been painted over, but that bike fit me perfectly and there was nothing I couldn't do on it. Navigating rocky, treacherous trails and oil-slick roads was easy as pie. I would spend hours riding my bike back and forth, parking it and swinging my legs over the seat to get off the bike like Ponch. Secretly I wished that Eric Estrada was my dad, and in my head I was convinced that there was a slight resemblance because of his brown skin colour. I must be related to him somehow! I fantasized that he would come rescue my sisters and me after being apart for so long, and that he was tremendously rich, with a roller rink in his house. I even tried to send a homemade letter fashioned out of red construction paper, but drawing a stamp on an envelope doesn't work and the mail woman brought it back to my house, much to my embarrassment. I was very relieved that my adoptive mother didn't open my letter to Eric Estrada proclaiming that I was his long-lost daughter and begging him to come rescue me.

The adventures my sisters and I went on always involved getting in trouble or someone getting hurt. From swimming across the lake to standing up in the canoes and rocking them until they tipped, our lives in the lake and outside of the house were fun. We were curious and precocious children, and thinking back to those days, we were afforded much more responsibility and opportunity than I would ever give my children today. I mean, at age eight I could tip a canoe in deep water and right it and climb back into it. I could start a fire unassisted, I knew how to bore a hole in the ice, put an old ice-fishing sinker on a line with a hook, and even clean a fish after I caught it. We were taught how to check if the ice was thick enough to walk on, how to pull a canoe out of the water and portage it across land and how to put it away on the rack. By ten I was pulling the canoe off the rack in the morning and paddling quietly across the lake with my fishing gear before the waves rippled the water. Mornings on the lake were my favourite time, and listening to the loons and seeing the fog hanging over the shining, glass-smooth water is my best memory. I had no fear of drowning; in fact, it never even crossed my mind until I was in my thirties.

I don't remember Scott doing anything remotely as dangerous as we girls did. Once when my sisters and I went hiking, we packed a lunch and headed off into the bush with no direction; we just wanted to explore. We lived in a heavily wooded area with many foothills and cliffs, and we ventured so far that we came to a place we had never been before. While climbing on a cliff, my sister Gina lost her footing and fell, and if she hadn't caught herself on a branch she would've fallen at least sixty feet. We laughed it off because, as children, we believed we were invincible. Gina would even tease us for worrying a little bit. I guess my point is that our life growing up doesn't seem all that bad, but this is just skimming the surface. These are things that most people saw: three girls who seemed happy, well adjusted, adventurous and healthy. What they didn't see was the pain, trauma and suffering that we endured living under that roof with those people.

I can't remember why I got my first beating. All I remember is being over Ronald's lap and him spanking me so hard I peed my pants. I screamed and begged for him to stop. Then he shoved me off his lap to the ground. My sisters cowered as they watched it happen. I remember my ass stinging so hard I couldn't sit down at first. I was wearing white tights and a navy blue wool dress. I had soaked my tights with urine, and after being shoved to the ground, I took off those soiled tights and crawled into bed to hide under my blankets. I was in shock and remember feeling fear creeping into my heart for the first time.

For years afterwards the beatings were given for things like bad grades, not putting away the silverware properly, not sweeping the floor properly, failing a test, forgetting homework, not cleaning our room, and sometimes we got beaten just because my dad was mean and felt like taking it out on someone. We would get kicked, hit with the belt across the butt, but mostly smacked 'til we pissed our pants. We always pissed our pants and screamed bloody murder, and my mother never helped us or offered us any consolation. In fact, my mother would report to my father when he got home from work; she was the bearer of bad news. Sometimes, if Ronald got home from his 3–11 p.m. shift and didn't like how the floor was swept, he would wake us up and make us do it again.

I cannot tell you how many times I cowered in my closet or in the front hall closet, trying to will myself invisible so that I didn't have to hear my father or be around him when he got angry or when I was in trouble. Supper was a stressful time in our house. Ronald sat at his designated spot at the head of the table, to his right sat Scott, and then Mary, myself, Gina, and

Dakota sat directly to Ronald's left. If she needed to get up to get something or be excused, it was excruciating for her. He was constantly grabbing her under the table, grabbing her knees, trying to fondle her, or if he wasn't trying to molest her he was insulting her by calling her "ugly," a "fat chiggaboo," or a "leper." (Dakota had a skin problem that caused her skin to show white patches in the summer. It was an allergic reaction to the sun, but after the first breakout Scott and Ronald teased her constantly, referring to her as a "leper.") I would see my sister squirm and giggle uncomfortably, but if Dakota protested Ronald's fumbling fingers, she would face his wrath. Maybe that's why she seemed so lost and disconnected: because she suffered so much in silence. How does a young girl deal with that much anger and humiliation being directed at her from her own family?

I know that my sisters and I feared Ronald because his beatings were so severe. His insults and temper tantrums were reminiscent of a movie I once watched called *Life with Billy*, about a woman's abusive relationship with her violent husband. Ronald was a cruel and sadistic man who would lose his temper at the drop of a hat, and when he did I would see his face turn bright red, even into his scalp. Ronald White was an original ginger, complete with bright red hair that grew in a widow's peak, a red moustache, freckles and pale white skin that would burn bright red in the summer. For some strange reason when he was doing physical activity, he would move his mouth like he was chewing gum, and I would stare at him because I thought it was the weirdest thing I'd ever seen. I never dared ask him why he did that. One time I dared to call him by his name, Ronald, rather than "dad." I thought I was being clever and funny but apparently there's a rule that no one tells kids about until they call their parents by their first name. I was slapped across the face, given a tongue lashing and embarrassed, and it was the kind of tongue lashing that left me hanging my head in shame, wanting to sink into the ground from humiliation. He was verbally abusive and it is a trait I picked up from him and carried into my adulthood.

I think the first beating scarred me for life, but it was one particular beating I received that proved to me that no one could help me or rescue me from my father. It taught me that he was truly a monster capable of anything. I was about five years old, playing outside with my sisters. We lived in the country and there was a fair amount of snow, so much that the banks would be six feet high and my sisters and I would make snow forts and dig tunnels. We also used to slide down the side facing away from the road with our plastic sliding sheets. One particular day my parents were shovelling the driveway and there was a big snow grader coming to plow the road. I was so terrified I could not move — the grader looked like a giant lobster ready to attack me. The grader was beeping a warning and had an orange light that went around in a circle, but I was frozen in my footsteps. My parents were yelling at me to hurry and cross the road to their side and I could not move. On top of this, I began to cry from fear because the grader was less than ten feet away and was just waiting for me to cross the road. My father was so angry he marched across the road and kicked me in the ass. I fell down and he kept kicking me until I got back up on my feet and finished crossing the road. I had urinated in my snowsuit and was absolutely traumatized. Why didn't the grader operator or my mother help me? How can people stand by and watch a man beat a small child?

After that event I was immediately sent inside to bed for being a big crybaby. To this day I am afraid of gravel graders and snow plows; I will cross the street or hide in buildings to avoid them when I am outside. I have even had my son hold my hand so I can walk beside one with my eyes closed. In a way it sounds ridiculous and funny, but it was a seriously traumatizing event in my life.

# CHAPTER 2

## Tasoosiw

BY THE TIME I was five and going to kindergarten, I was a head banger. Not the metal-head, rock star kind of head banger but a serious wall head banger. I would bang my head mercilessly against my bedroom wall and rock myself to sleep — or maybe I was knocking myself out. I did this nightly for most of my childhood and even into my teens and early adult life. I was very ashamed of my head banging and felt it carried the same shame as being caught masturbating or stealing. The shame and anxiety I carried into my adulthood about being a head banger finally subsided after I dealt with the reasons why I did it and alleviated the shame through therapy. But growing up in my house, banging my head against the wall brought on morning beatings that I will remember for the rest of my life. As a head banger I wasn't very aware or conscious I was doing it; sometimes I would put myself to sleep with it, others times I would wake up in the morning and bang my head to put myself back to sleep. One particular morning, I must have been banging my head in my sleep because I woke my father up. He came into my room and started pummelling my head and body with his fists. He was yelling and very angry that my head banging had woken him up.

Did I stop head banging? No, I just did it more quietly. I can tell you that my head banging was so severe that I wrecked the drywall, which then needed to be repaired, so I was given a giant stuffed dog to buffer the area between the wall and my head. It didn't work and eventually my father put a 2'x 6" plank against the wall to deter my head banging. At no time did anyone show concern or take me to a doctor to see if I had brain damage or emotional problems. I started using the dresser adjacent to my bed. It was harder but effective; in fact, I think the first few times I knocked myself out. It was only later in my life that I learned I banged my head to deal with the stress, trauma and loneliness I experienced as a child. This is very hard to talk about for me because of the shame and guilt I still feel in connection to that time. I would bang my head when I was bored, lonely, angry, sad or stressed. As a teenager I would bang my head into my pillow, and my friends teased me constantly.

I continued to bang my head in adulthood but I learned to do it privately — or so I thought, because my children were witnessing it without really knowing what I was doing. As they grew and became aware of what their mom was doing, they began to ask questions. They even made fun of me, not to be cruel but because they thought it funny to see their mother acting crazy. I was mortified that my children had seen me banging my head into my pillow and became very discreet about it. I believe it was in 2004 or 2005 when I finally quit altogether because my kids were too old, but also because I was getting terrible headaches from it. To this day I fear I damaged my brain somehow, though maybe not since I am still able to function. I have learned so much and hope it's not too late to change the things that have affected my parenting and how I deal with relationships.

~ ~ ~

It wasn't until I was older that I realized I grew up in a household where my sisters and I were treated not like family but like second-class citizens, like live-in help. Some of the differences were subtle and I distinctly remember asking my mother why she, Scott and Ronald got butter and us girls had to eat margarine, or why they ate white bread and we ate brown. I was in grade four and recall a classmate making fun of my brown bread sandwiches, telling me my skin was brown because I ate brown bread. I hadn't realized my brown skin was different, I just thought I tanned well in the summer. I was so angry that I went home to demand my mother let me have white bread sandwiches with peanut butter and jelly like the other kids and Scott. Not once did anyone tell me I was Indigenous or explain to me why my skin was brown.

I always felt that my adoptive brother Scott was trusted more than we were. He was never spanked, hit, beaten or grounded in the whole time I lived in that house. Nor did he have to clean, vacuum, dust or do dishes or laundry. My father never raised his voice at Scott and he never got in trouble for anything.

The difference that stands out the most to me was using the outhouse in the middle of the night during the coldest times of the year. Our pipes would freeze regularly every winter and we were forced to use the outhouse — but only my sisters and me. My parents and Scott used an indoor port-a-potty, the chemical kind that would sit in the bathroom. I was reminded of the difference in our household between my sisters and I and my parents and brother when I saw a movie recently called *The Help*, about the civil rights movement in the U.S. in the 1960s. The Black women who worked in the white people's houses and cared for their children were not allowed to use the toilets inside the home. Instead they were forced to use separate washrooms, sometimes located outside, and they would sneak into the white employer's toilets if there was an emergency. I was reminded of a time when I snuck into the bathroom to use it discreetly because it was so cold outside and I hated sitting on the frozen toilet seat. I never did get caught but my parents suspected that we girls were sneaking a pee in their precious toilet. Oh how I dreamed of taking an indoor piss during those winter months. And peeing and pooping at school was a luxury. My sisters were protective of me, so if I woke up in the middle of the night, one of them would come with me to the outhouse and stay with me while I peed. As a child my imagination would get the best of me and I thought the "shitmonster" who lived in the bottom was going to come up through the outhouse hole to get me.

The one beautiful thing about being outside in the middle of the night waiting for each other to pee was seeing the moon light up and reflect across the frozen lake, and watching the snow glistening like diamonds across the yard. But I swore as a grownup that I would never use another outhouse as long as I lived.

My parents kept an extra key hanging in the outhouse for the days they were not home after school. If we used the key and did not put it back outside in the shed, we were locked out. Sometimes my sisters and I would break into the house by climbing into the windows; other times we would sit outside and wait, or wait in the rabbit shed because at least it was a covered shed with some protection from the cold. The shed stank horribly but it kept us sheltered for an hour or so. Sometimes I would get locked out of the house and instead of freezing in the cold outhouse, I would pee in the rabbit shed. I felt so dirty for doing it but I rationalized that with all the rabbit shit and piss in the shed, no one would even notice. And no one ever did.

Most kids are happy to see their parents get home from work or outings, but dread always crept into my stomach when I saw the car pull into the driveway. I never knew what to expect from Ronald; would he be in a good mood and drunk or in a bad mood? If Ronald came home in a good mood there were treats to be had and we didn't have to tiptoe around waiting for him to blow his top over the smallest thing. The thing was, we never knew what the blow-up was going to be about. It could be about anything, from supper being late to the driveway not being shovelled properly, or it could be about our pigsty of a room. It was never about Scott's room though.

The only time I recognized Ronald being in a good mood was when he drank beer. Occasionally when us kids accompanied our adoptive parents on trips to town for groceries, we would be treated to Kentucky Fried Chicken or Purple Lantern, which was a Chinese food restaurant. Then afterwards, on the way home, Ronald would stop at the Navel Vets, which was a bar in the basement of a building. Us kids would sit upstairs in a small hallway and wait while our parents drank beer, sometimes for hours. Sometimes my mother would come upstairs and assure us that we would be leaving soon. Back then you could smoke anywhere inside and clouds of blue smoke wafted up the stairs. I rationalized the gruelling hours of waiting with "it was the least we could do for our father who had just treated us to Kentucky Fried Chicken." I never thought about drinking and driving because we always made it home safe, but yes, my father always drove the twenty-five kilometres home on a rural highway drunk. Lord knows how many beers he'd had downstairs in the bar; he never staggered but he was definitely happier.

When he drank at home, he was playful but mean. One evening he held me down and tickled me until I screamed and cried, then he pushed me away roughly and called me a baby. I never wanted him to play with me again because I was so afraid he would tickle me and hold me down. Being tickled until you scream and beg for mercy is cruel and I don't care if it starts out as fun. When a child is crying and begging for mercy, an adult needs to stop. To this day I cannot stand to be tickled by anyone, in fact I have quite a violent reaction if someone attempts to tickle me. It's a survivor instinct. I punch and kick on reflex and try to get away from the person initiating the grabbing. Most people think I'm joking when I tell them that I do not like tickling and that I will fight back violently.

Sometimes Ronald was a terrible drunk. One time he was trying to fix something in the house and not being very successful. He started yelling and cursing at my mother, who was trying to cook and help him at the same time. He flew into a rage and chased her around with a cast iron frying pan. I ran into the front hall but I also grabbed a pot to protect myself. I remember there was a chair in the front hall and I squeezed myself between the chair and the wall, armed with my pot. I could hear my father screaming and yelling and my mom yelling, "Stop it, Ronald!" It was over as quickly as it began. There was silence so I came out from hiding and crept around to find my sisters. I was secretly praying that they had found a place to hide also. I knew Scott was safe and that he would never be in danger from his father.

This incident caused Mary to take us girls and leave Ronald. She told us to pack our swimsuits. My sisters and I were confused and scared. We fled in the station wagon to town. My mom took us to the Queen Elizabeth pool for a family swim and then to see a movie. It was a great night. I think she was trying to keep us busy while she decided what to do, because the next thing I knew we were at my Aunty Sarah's house, Mary's sister. Sarah made beds for us in her basement and I remember wishing we could live there and never go back. But alas, we did go back and my mother never tried to rescue herself or us again.

I never did like my aunties; I found them condescending, uncaring and bossy. They always had a load of unsolicited advice and constantly pointed out how much weight us girls had gained. I knew at an early age that these aunties would give me no comfort: I could not run into their arms, happy to see them or to seek protection from my father, even though they knew he was a bad man. They had their own marriages and problems to worry about, although I don't think their husbands beat their children. But growing up I thought all kids got beaten.

I have to admit, I did benefit from the arduous labour in that household because it taught me a valuable work ethic. I am not afraid to roll up my sleeves and get my hands dirty. My sisters and I were strong girls. One summer Ronald decided to build an extension on the trailer-house. He wanted to add a garage with two bedrooms upstairs. The previous fall he had demolished our existing bedrooms and we'd slept in the front hall for months, my eldest sister on a mattress on the floor. The cement foundation for the garage was laid and in the spring we began to work. Ronald didn't hire men to come help him; he had three unpaid child labourers to do his heavy work.

We never worked so hard in our lives — building and hanging trusses, lifting heavy pieces of siding, and hell would break loose if we broke one. They were long and bendy and sometimes would snap if they weren't supported properly in the middle. We installed insulation, laid shingles, hung heavy drywall sheets, and after all that, we got to pick the colour of our bedroom's walls before we primed and painted them. On one particular afternoon, while we were installing insulation, I began to complain how tired and hot it was and how a swim in the lake would help us work harder. Ronald called me a baby and sent me to bed without supper. Later on I heard my siblings splashing around in the lake. I never complained again after that. By the time I went back to school in the fall, I was so dark, tanned and muscular that my classmates were admiring my legs and arms. The calves of my legs were huge, my arms well defined. At twelve years old I was more muscular than any boy in my classroom.

That same summer, our parents took us on a road trip across the midwestern United States, our destination being the west coast of Washington. I remember there was a *TripTik* map from the Canadian Automobile Association that showed every stop along the way, so you couldn't possibly get lost. We stopped at every single damned historical site on the route. Ronald and Scott loved historical sites and would stand and stare at funny statues of old men or visit rickety museums on backcountry roads. To curb my boredom along the way, I would visit the bathrooms of each establishment, except for the outhouses. Most of the time I genuinely needed to use the toilet but I was also curious as to how other people lived and decorated their bathrooms.

Mary had a hard time navigating that *TripTik* map; even with the trip highlighted in yellow we would still make a wrong turn and Ronald would fly into a rage at the wheel. He would threaten to drive the car off the road into a tree. Can you imagine being a child in the back seat of a station wagon, wedged between your brother and sister, listening to this raging bull driving and threatening to kill us all because he'd gotten lost? There was no tuning him out, no hiding or running away, so we'd be forced to listen and tolerate his tantrums. It was terrifying and really put a damper on the eight-hour drive to another historical site.

The most memorable part of this trip was that my sister Gina was with me, and she was funny as heck. Dakota had stayed behind to volunteer in some sporting event. When we stopped to rest for the night, we often stayed in campgrounds. We would set the tents up, which was another rage session for Ronald. No matter how many times we set up the tents during that trip, he would always forget how to do it and then throw camp equipment around, or at us, screaming about how stupid we were. After a while we got used to his rages, and knowing he wouldn't hit us in public, we would snicker or give each other knowing looks of exasperation.

My favourite memories of this trip are buying a rattlesnake-tail necklace with my allowance and visiting Yellowstone National Park. We stayed in a campsite called Roosevelt Lodge Cabins in the foothills of the mountains. This campsite was like the Old West you see on television, with rustic cabins, horse-back trails, even a corral, and with a big common hall and bar for tourists. Gina and I explored every inch of the property. We walked on the trails until we saw signs warning tourists that grizzly bears had been spotted in the area and were attracted to food and to menstruating women, then we turned around and went back to the tourist area. Later that day we met two teenage boys who said they were from Los Angeles and played in a rock band. They were brothers named Gino and Oscar and they both had brown skin like us. They seemed to be about Gina's age, fifteen. We agreed to meet them after supper on a little foothill overlooking the cabins and fields. Gina shared a smoke with one of the boys but I distinctly remember Oscar talking to me and showing a lot of interest in me. Boys hadn't even interested me until that evening; playing hockey and competing in sports were the only things I knew boys could do besides be a nuisance. Kissing a boy was not something that had crossed my mind, probably because I was only twelve years old.

As we were sitting on this little foothill at a picnic table, smoking cigarettes and listening to music on a little portable boombox, we suddenly smelled something terrible, like manure, which caused us to look around for the source. Out in the field we could see a dark shape moving towards us, and it was a bison! All the warning signs on the way into Yellowstone Park had said that bison were known for charging and even goring tourists. We ran down the hill and back to the common area in the campsite to find our parents. As we were running, Oscar grabbed my hand, causing me to stop. He put a hand around my waist, turned me around, and French kissed me until my legs went weak and started to buckle. Then all of a sudden it was over and he took off back to his own cabin. We never saw those particular boys again but it stirred something inside me and boy craziness took over. The next morning my family packed up to leave and our parents told us the warden had warned campers about a bison walking around in the cabin areas.

Gina was fearless and would talk with strangers and make friends so easily, everywhere we went. I was the tag-along, annoying little sister, but I admired her so much. One day we stayed in a cabin area in a different part of Yellowstone National Park. We took a walk to the top of a hill and just sat there looking out at the beautiful landscape with the Rocky Mountains as the backdrop. We talked about our dreams, about boys, what our friends in Sault Ste. Marie were doing, and how much we missed the lake, Dakota and our dog. All of a sudden Gina motioned for me to be quiet. She pointed to my left side — very close to us was a deer grazing on the grass. We didn't move a muscle and watched it chew and eventually move away from us, but we felt like something magical had happened, just for us.

My parents decided not to go all the way to the West Coast so we went to some big canyon and turned around. On the way back we stopped in a placed called Custer's Last Stand. My sister and I had no idea of the significance of this place; to us it was just dusty and boring. My parents didn't explain anything but they seemed really focused on this Custer guy. There was no apparent association with Indigenous people or what the land meant, just rows and rows of white crosses, a small museum and no custard to be had! Later on in life, I would learn the significance of this place and it made sense that my parents would focus on the loss of the settler soldiers instead of on the Lakota, Northern Cheyenne and Arapaho tribes' victory that day. We headed back home and that was to be the last significant amount of time I spent with my sister Gina before she ran away.

# CHAPTER 3

# Môniy'w

Throughout my life I've always been successfully employed, or as I like to refer to it, successfully assimilated. I gained a trillion skills that would later get me through tough times but the survival skills I learned are the ones that stay forever. Those are hard to put away. It's a lot of work being on guard all the time and posturing a mindset of toughness that maybe isn't working so well anymore. Can anyone really shut that off at will?

I grew up not knowing my adoptive mother was First Nations as she was very pale-skinned and had blue eyes. She was born on a local First Nations reserve to a white mother and an Ojibway father. When Mary married and moved off reserve to live with Ronald, she lost her Indian status. She regained it some time in the 90s when she divorced him and moved back on reserve. To this day I'm not sure if she divorced him because he wasn't allowed to live on the reserve with her or because he cheated on her, but I do know that she didn't divorce him after he was charged with three counts of sexual indecency and gross indecency against my sisters. No, she stood by her pedophile husband and never whispered a word to her family.

There was a huge disparity between how us girls and our adoptive brother were treated. As a child I could not speak out or even identify that my sisters and I were treated differently than our adoptive brother. It's a hurtful feeling to know you are not valued as much as your light-skinned brother, I thought he must have been pretty special. Scott never knew the sting on his ass after a harsh spanking, nor did he have to change his pants after pissing himself from fear. Scott never went to bed terrified, crying and lonely. Scott never knew the cold outhouse on a late school night or pissing in the rabbit shed because he was locked out of the house. Scott has always known comfort, convenience and the privilege of being born "white," to "white" parents. A thin wall separated our rooms but a massive wall of privilege separated our experiences in that household.

I watched my parents support and encourage Scott to excel. He flourished while my sisters and I ran from Ronald's abusive, wandering hands. My brother had a job, lived at home, had his own car and attended college. Was I jealous? No, I was deeply hurt that we were not valued in the same way and not afforded the same opportunities. Instead my sisters and I lived in fear of a father who molested us. I felt angry and helpless. I could not speak out against the atrocities that I witnessed for fear that I would hurt my mother or put her in danger. But it was a torn loyalty I had, and still have, for my mother because she never showed that she cared for me or loved me as a child or even as an adult.

The first time I discovered that my mother kept our abuse a secret was in October 1998. I had fled Edmonton with my three children, Cree, Charmaine and Jonathan, and was staying in an old house on my adoptive mother's property because we were not allowed to stay in her house. The old house only had cold running water and each night the floor was mysteriously covered with hundreds of dead blackflies. We took our meals at my mother's and slept on the floor in the old house. I was grateful somewhat to be away from Edmonton but the quietness of the night scared me and kept me awake. There were no sirens, no background dirty noise to comfort me, just — nothing. I was tremendously lonely and wondered if I had made a big mistake by moving back to Sault Ste. Marie.

My mother's sister Allison was visiting one day and asked me, quite directly, "Why exactly did you leave Sault Ste. Marie? Mary told us you wanted to party and be with boys." It all made sense to me then, why my adoptive mother's family spoke to me condescendingly and why they hadn't been very friendly or welcoming since my return. Mary had told her family that us girls left to party and be promiscuous and never revealed what her husband had done to us.

I never did want to return to Sault Ste. Marie but it was the only place that I knew to go. I had no one and nowhere to go and I was fleeing abuse, in the grips of alcohol addiction and terribly broke. I imagined a wonderful reunion with my mother, who was now divorced, and thought that I'd settle into some sort of normalcy. But once again she treated me like a second-class citizen and my warm, fuzzy dream of us having another chance at family faded.

I learned that I could not talk to my mother about anything personal or intimate because she and I did not have that type of relationship. For reasons I don't fully understand, I had respect for my mother. I never smoked or swore in front of her, I followed the rules in her house and did my best to keep her house clean when we did laundry or cooked. I made sure to call her weekly after we moved out and kept her updated on the kids' activities. At times she would help me when I needed rides to get groceries or go to appointments but I learned not to ask for more than five or ten dollars. One time in 1999, I called my mother after moving into an apartment with my young children. I had virtually no groceries and was frying potatoes for the kids for breakfast and then again for lunch. I called to ask her for money to buy lunchmeat and snacks for the kids. She brought me over a small bag of homemade cookies and that was all. My heart sank as I realized I could not rely on my mother for financial or emotional help. I didn't feel like she owed me anything but I did want to feel that she cared about us.

I also wanted to feel trusted. I don't think my adoptive mother ever trusted me and maybe she had her reasons not to. In the past my sisters and I had lied to her to avoid physical punishment. At one point I even pawned a keyboard she had bought me. I needed diapers and food more than I needed a keyboard. A mother will do whatever it takes to keep her kids' bellies full. I had sold and pawned so many things in my life and I knew I could easily do without them. But I believe I hurt my mother by pawning that keyboard. She will never understand that the day before I left Edmonton, I had to sell the keyboard to escape my abusive husband. I guess that is why my mother never trusted me again with money or belongings. From that day forward, she sent me a jar of homemade jam or homemade items for Christmas and one time a set of pots and pans — she must have figured out that it's hard to pawn pots and pans.

Growing up in the White household, it seemed that respect and encouragement were extended to Scott unequivocally; he could do no wrong. I believe the kind of support he received helped him succeed in life. The conditions and abuses that my sisters and I and many 60s Scoop survivors endured have led to lives of continued abuse and struggles to heal. This is the legacy of the 60s Scoop.

I have worked hard to heal and to build a productive life and through it all, have had no support or recognition from my adoptive family. My daughter has heard the negative comments about me, even while I was working as a Peer Support Worker for the Program for Assertive Community Treatment team at Sault Area Hospital. I was gainfully employed and had been sober for twelve years but there was no acknowledgement of my accomplishments. There has also been no acknowledgement that the hardships my sisters and I endured in childhood contributed to the problems we carried into our young adult lives. I believe our years in the White house left us unable to cope, seeking abusive partners, and using drugs and alcohol to forget the pain and suffering we had endured.

My adoptive mother refuses to accept how our lives have turned out and continues to maintain that we are responsible for the choices we made. At fifteen, my sisters and I fled an abusive household full of physical and sexual violence, sought refuge with friends and never went back for fear of being punished. Years before, when I was around nine or ten, my sisters and I had tried to flee. We had decided we were going to run away to the Children's Aid Society (CAS) and believed they would help us, rescue us even, and find us a new home. The school we attended had buses that travelled the twenty-five kilometres from Sault Ste. Marie to where we lived, did their school runs and then went back to the bus bay in town. My sisters and I stayed on the bus one day and got off in town. It was the first and only time I had ever been in town on my own and I was terrified. We went to CAS and sat in the lobby waiting to speak to a worker. They did not listen to us when we said our father beat us, and instead they brought us back to the White household. My sisters and I were beaten and grounded for telling and for going into town on the bus.

On another occasion when we tried to run away, we had been piling wood after school. We didn't even put our books and bags away, we just started working as soon as we entered the yard. My father showed us how to pile the wood and we began to work. My friend Carla helped us stack the wood and after completing the woodpile, my father came out to inspect it. He said the pile was crooked and began to throw chunks of wood at us, big chunks that hit our legs and backs. We ran screaming out of the yard and up the road. We hid in the bushes by Carla's house, which was about two kilometres further down the road, and we built a lean-to fort from pine boughs and lined the floor with moss. Dakota and I were crying, cold and scared that Ronald was going to come find us — can you imagine having that much fear that your father is going to severely hurt you or kill you?

Gina was a rock and our fearless leader; she told us stories and kept our spirits up. We stayed in that lean-to shelter until dark and were prepared to stay all night if we had to. I did not want to go home. Carla brought some oranges and bread from her house and told us Ronald had called her dad and told him to send us home. We cried and were terrified to go home and get beaten. Eventually we did go home and we were sent to bed. I fell asleep right away and the event was never mentioned again.

The day my sister Gina ran away, she had gotten into trouble for not standing up her bike, but this time she spoke back to my father, who then punched her in the stomach. Gina fell to the ground, her breath knocked out of her, and Ronald fell to the ground begging her to get up. Gina yelled at him that she was going to tell on him and afterwards we sisters gathered around in a group in the bedroom. Gina promised that she would come back to get us and that we would be sent to live with a nice, rich foster family, maybe even our own parents! She ran away that night. When she didn't come back to sleep and didn't come home from school the next day, I pretended that I didn't know she had planned to run away and couldn't possibly know where she was. She moved in with my childhood friend Carla's family down the road, and after that she moved in with my mother's sister Allison, who lived in town. Allison objected to Gina leaving hair in the sink and had other petty complaints so my sister moved into a home for teenage girls. I would visit her on occasion but she didn't do well there either.

Gina eventually moved to Toronto and we got word that she

was working the streets as a sex worker. I was angry that she never came back for me and I felt betrayed. I didn't care that she was working as a prostitute, in fact I imagined her being as street-smart and tough as the character in this movie called *Angel*, about a fifteen-year-old prostitute. Dakota moved out shortly afterwards and found refuge with her friend Trixie's family, who were moderately wealthy and owned several hair salons. Dakota eventually moved into town and met Steve, and then became pregnant with his baby.

Dakota and Steve were living together and she seemed to be doing all right considering she was only seventeen, but looks are deceiving. Steve was physically and emotionally abusive to Dakota. He smoked a lot of weed and was stoned most of the time I was there. Steve once tried to convince me that Dakota was possessed by a demon. Later that night they got into a physical fight, which led me to intervene and beg Dakota to leave him. Dakota sided with Steve and I was not allowed back there again. A month or so later Dakota ended up getting her own place in a rooming house with a hotplate, but that must have been lonely for her. She eventually moved into Women in Crisis, a shelter for abused women. I felt relieved she had somewhere to stay. For Christmas I bought her a frying pan and underwear from BiWay. Dakota laughed at these gifts but it had taken me forever to pick them out and I'd only had eight dollars.

Later on I heard that Gina had moved to Edmonton with her new boyfriend Floyd, that she was pregnant with his child and that they were getting married in Floyd's parents' house. Floyd's family was Portuguese and wealthy. Gina was approximately seven months pregnant when she got married. She gave birth to Cheyenne shortly after that, on April 9, 1988. I was still living at home and I remember my parents making arrangements to send flowers to the hospital where she had delivered.

My time in that household after my sisters moved out was very lonely. Scott had gone away for school and my mother was taking computer classes in the evenings. Sports were over for me; I had suffered a major knee injury playing basketball, which had me on crutches for eight weeks. I began to drink beer with my friends when we could find it, and smoke cigarettes. My father's advances towards me became more aggressive. I think I should backtrack here to when I began to notice that things were not right.

Ronald had roaming hands and would try to fondle our breasts by leaning over our shoulders and grabbing. If we moved quickly enough he never got a chance. He was so brazen that he did it in the kitchen while we were helping our mother cook, and she would call him a "dirty old man" but never stop him. He would grab our asses and have us scurrying to get away from him. Ronald would sit on the toilet taking a shit while we washed ourselves in the bathtub and the only thing separating us was an opaque glass shower door. Believe me, that was not a big bathroom. I remember holding the shower door shut with one hand to make sure he wasn't trying to peek at me.

Ronald would come into our bedroom at night and he would linger at Dakota's bed. Her bunk was directly above mine. She would be giggling and her bed would be moving around and I thought that he was telling her bedtime stories and paying special attention to her. I could not imagine what else they could be doing and I was jealous that my sister was getting so much attention. As an adult I learned that Ronald had been sexually molesting Dakota right in her bed. This came out in court and my heart dropped when I learned of what my sister endured.

Ronald had also molested Gina, a sordid story that died with her, since the grim details are hidden away in sealed court documents. She carried that burden with her — as a child and then as an adult — until her death. So Ronald was already a sexual predator when he started coming after me and making sexual suggestions.

I used to snoop through my parents' bedroom and found dirty magazines under his bed with sexually explicit stories that piqued my interest. As a teen going through puberty, I was curious. At my age, the act of sex was about Ken and Barbie rubbing their bumps together; I didn't know the penis went into the vagina or all the details of how it happened. I would steal the magazines and read them, trying to picture the words in my head, and then I'd try to put them back without getting caught. I was very curious about the "act of sex." Ronald must have noticed his collection was being tampered with. He questioned me one day in my bedroom about the books and if I enjoyed reading them and what I liked the most. I never touched his books again but his interest in me began to change and he would watch me go up the stairs in my nightgown, trying to steal a peek. He would also sometimes grab at my legs as I ascended the stairs. His hands were always trying to grab something. As younger girls, my sisters and I were forced to give Ronald backrubs, sometimes for hours, straddling his back and rubbing at his pimply skin until either he fell asleep or said we could go. Only my sisters and I were forced to give him backrubs. It was pure torture to sit on his back for an hour, rubbing at his skin until he was satisfied.

When I turned fifteen, Scott was away studying and my mother was taking more computer courses. One day Ronald said he wanted to talk to me later, when my mother wouldn't be home. That evening I went to meet him on the front porch, having no idea what he could want from me. He asked me if I was taking birth control or if I'd been having sex and I said no, which was the truth. I had only kissed and done some heavy petting with a local boy. Ronald then asked if he could be my first! He said that a father should be a daughter's first. I told him that no, it wasn't okay because he was my father and that's not allowed. Ronald said it would be okay because we weren't related by blood, but that we would have to be careful that I didn't get pregnant and not to tell my mom. Ronald asked me to think about it and to keep it our secret. I remember my ears ringing and the sounds of waves swooshing in my head. I think it was fear and shock and disgust. I kept that secret for a few weeks and even admittedly used it against my father, bribing him to buy my friends and me beer. Little did they know why my dad bought me beer.

During this time my father's sexual advances became more brazen and he kept pushing me to decide whether I was going to have sex with him or not. One particular evening he told me that I better be ready because he was getting impatient. I was starting to worry that I might actually have to have sex with him.

That evening my friends and I went out and we ended up getting drunk in the bush. When we arrived home my father was yelling at us as we crawled up the stairs, drunk and giggling. I didn't get grounded but later, as the alcohol wore off, I began weeping on my bed and confessed to my friend Carla what my father had asked me. She was so upset and disgusted. Carla had come to stay with us for a few weeks due to her own family problems. She moved out the next day and went to stay with another friend, Nicky. She told Nicky's parents about the secret I had confided in her. They didn't know whether to believe her or not and said that they needed to hear it from me.

Carla met with me later that day to tell me that I could go to Nicky's parents to ask for help. I was angry and felt trapped. I didn't want my dad to get in trouble because I was afraid of what he might do to me. I certainly wanted to leave but I didn't want to leave my mother behind. That day or the next, before he went to work, my father told me that I better be ready because tonight he wanted sex while my mom was at school. He said he got condoms and he wasn't waiting any longer. I cannot tell you the fear that went into my heart; it was like a jolt of electricity and I began panicking, wondering what I was going to do. I felt backed into a corner, trapped — but then I remembered I could call Nicky's parents. I was lucky enough to reach them at their camp down the road. Bonnie and Leon were cleaning up their summer camp and heading to their permanent winter home and I had just reached them in time. They told me to pack what I could and they would be there to pick me up in ten minutes. I haphazardly packed some clothes and waited on the road, fearing that my dad or mom would come home at any second. I was terrified that Ronald would find me at Bonnie and Leon's place. I paced back and forth until Bonnie finally arrived. She had been very clear that if I was lying, she could not help me, but if I was telling the truth, she would protect me, and Ronald would never touch me again. I waited on pins and needles for Bonnie to call my parents to let them know I was with them. I remember her saying, "Colleen is staying with us now, and if you want to make waves — *we* can make waves, Ronald!" and hanging up. Bonnie was fearless.

I cried myself to sleep that night, unsure of my future and wanting to die from shame and humiliation. I felt dirty as a human being, I felt shame for telling on my dad, and I felt humiliated that I needed help and my secret was no longer mine. Nicky and her brother had to share their house and their parents with me. I was put into Nicky's room and I felt like an invader. I had never been this close to her or her family before. Normally I would just pick Nicky up from her camp and I had never really spent a large amount of time around her family. This was very different for me, living in a home where there was no fear and a sense of cocoon comfort.

Bonnie laid down the rules. I was told that I either had to work or go to school full time; I chose school. I was enrolled in an all-girls Catholic high school, which wasn't too bad at all. I made new friends right away and Nicky's friends welcomed me into their circle. I skipped out a lot and smoked pot occasionally but I was passing grade ten. One day in November, Bonnie showed up at my school and told me today was the day I was going to tell my story to the police and social workers. She drove me to Children's Aid, the same place that hadn't listened to us before, and brought me to a large conference room with two police officers and a few social workers. There was a tape recorder on the table and I began to tell them about every instance of abuse that my sisters and I had endured. I also told them how Ronald had propositioned me to be my first sexual partner. I know that my father was charged and after that it turned into a court case that involved my sisters. My sisters gave statements and Ronald was charged with sexual indecency, sexual interference and sexual assault. He was never charged for what he did to me but I was okay with that. If I'd never told on him he would have gotten away with it all.

~~~

Growing up in the White home we did not hug or kiss or show signs of affection to each other. Mary did not console us when we got hurt or were crying. I certainly did not know how to extend affection to anybody either, and any act of touching me triggered revulsion and retreat. Every night Nicky and her parents would kiss each other goodnight. I did not like this and it took a long time before I could do as they did, and even then it felt perverted. This discomfort would carry into my adult life and even now I have a hard time extending affection to my children and loved ones. During my young adult life and even as an adult woman I perceived sex and affection as the same thing. What I craved the most was unconditional support and affection from a father. I didn't understand why after I slept with a man that he didn't love me and I had more than enough promiscuous sex seeking that love, which I never found.

~~~

I lived with Nicky's family for eight months, from September 1988 to March 1989. I gave them a fair share of trouble with drinking, missing curfew, smoking and skipping school but I never got hit and I didn't have to worry about roaming hands. I lost my virginity in a hotel bathroom on the shower floor with a drunken loser I never saw again.

One night my friends and I were at a house party with many adults. I began showing off by attempting to drink a concoction of hard liquor and beer. About twenty minutes later, as I sat on the couch, I began vomiting forcefully at least four feet across the room, much to the dismay of Nicky, who was sitting beside me. I remember seeing her reaction out of the corner of my eye as the vomit started flying out of my mouth uncontrollably. She was trying to get away from me and I was trying to keep the vomit in my mouth, which made quite a mess. It kept coming out and anyone in the way got sprayed as I ran to the bathroom, trying to get to the sink. My friend Carla was in the bathroom with the door closed, making out with her boyfriend, and vomit was hitting the door.

The next thing I knew, I was hanging over the sink puking my guts out and crying because it wouldn't stop. I could have died in that bathroom. I don't remember much after that until I woke up on the floor of a bedroom and heard the adults saying they were going to throw me outside in the snowbank.

I passed out again and awoke to Bonnie screaming at the adults about giving alcohol to minors. Then she was hauling me off the ground, yelling at me to get my boots on, and by this time I was just drunk and not sick. I was giggling and fell over trying to put my boots on. I didn't know that Carla and Nicky had walked three kilometres home in the freezing cold. They woke Bonnie up at one in the morning to come and get me because I was so drunk. They were so mad at me and I was giggling all the way home in the truck while Bonnie yelled at me. The next day I was not hung over but I did get grounded for the next two weeks, until the day I left for Edmonton.

The event that led me to catch a bus to Edmonton was Gina finding out that I had run away from home. I don't know how she found out; it may have been when she was contacted by the Edmonton police to give a statement for the court case against Ronald. When Gina found out that I might have been molested or hurt by Ronald, she went into a frenzy. She told her husband in Edmonton that she was going to hitchhike to Sault Ste. Marie to get me. I was able to call my sister from Nicky's house, though long distance cost a lot of money back in those days. We didn't have a very long conversation but we did agree I was going to move to Edmonton by March break. I remember telling Bonnie I wanted to quit school and leave on March break. She was very angry and tried to convince me to stay until the summer but I refused to listen to reason. I declared that if she forced me to stay, I would run away and hitchhike to Edmonton.

Bonnie finally gave in and plans began to bring me to Edmonton. I was also happy to find out my sister had combed the streets of Edmonton in search of our biological parents, and had found them. My biological father, Ricky, had learned that I was trying to come out to Edmonton and sent money for a bus ticket through my sister Gina. The money never did make it to me, and Bonnie and Leon ended up paying for my one-way bus ticket plus giving me $50 for the three-day journey. Bonnie had been serious about grounding me for drinking. Right up until the day I left for Edmonton, I was only allowed to leave the house to go to school. It was March 26, 1989, and I was sixteen.

# CHAPTER 4

## Tapasiiwin

I LEFT ON THE midnight Greyhound for Edmonton. Carla and Nicky came into town to catch the bus with me for a short part of the journey. They rode with me for the fifteen kilometres to where Nicky lived along Highway 17 and then they were dropped off. We all cried and hugged goodbye on the bus and I watched them through the window, waving as I rode away into the unknown. I cried all the way to Wawa, which was about two hours. I wasn't scared at all; if anything, I was excited, but leaving the familiar was hard. This would be one of the many times I uprooted myself to start over. It was the beginning of my running.

My journey lasted three days and I ate chips and chocolate bars and drank chocolate milk throughout. It was the longest, most boring ride but it was also an adventure. I was unafraid of people and thought it was pretty darn awesome being on my own with no rules or expectations. I remember pulling into downtown Edmonton and seeing how flat the land was and staring up and out the windows of the bus at the tall buildings, which blocked out the sun. My sister was waiting for me when I got off the bus, and her husband Floyd was holding Cheyenne. We hugged and cried and afterwards made the journey to her apartment in the basement of a house. It was clean and modern.

I don't know what I expected — maybe I thought Gina would be living in a shack. My sister laughed when I asked what was for supper and then she said, "White bread and Kool-Aid." I was seriously worried for a minute but then realized she had been joking. Gina joked around a lot. I had a really hard time understanding Floyd when I first met him; he stuttered with every word and his head bobbed, and I thought he was choking. I had to concentrate so hard on not laughing that I barely understood what my brother-in-law was talking about. After supper Floyd rolled a joint — he didn't stutter as much when he was high — and we all had a few hoots and went to West Edmonton Mall. This mall had a theme park in it with a roller coaster and rides. I was in heaven and in that moment I thought life couldn't get any better.

After we visited West Edmonton Mall we stopped at my biological father's apartment. I was so excited to meet my dad, but I didn't know I had a half-brother also. My dad was a short man and I was the spitting image of him. We hugged and talked a little. I met my brother Lucky, who was about ten years old then and a very large boy. At this time I remember not trusting men, so as much as I wanted a relationship with my dad, I could not bring myself to let my guard down enough to get close to him.

The very next day I met my biological mother, Esther, and her brother, my Uncle Marvin. I had never seen a person so drunk. My mother smelled toxic, a strong chemical smell like Lysol. They were both trying to navigate the basement stairs but they ended up falling because Uncle Marvin, who was trying to help her stand, was also drunk. *This is not how I imagined meeting my mother.* Once she laid eyes on me she began crying and hugging me, hanging all over me and suffocating me with the smell of Lysol. My mother was of average height, with a slim build and a small bulge on her stomach. She wasn't attractive nor was she ugly, but I didn't see one bit of resemblance between us. She kept calling me "baby" as an endearing term because I was the baby among her girls. I was so disappointed and felt my heart sink; after all that we had been through, I wanted a mother to hold me, comfort me and let me cry on her shoulder. I wanted my mother to tell me she had been looking for us and things were going to be better now. I wanted a mother whose lap I could sit on and hug her until I was all cried out. This was not the reunion I had fantasized about. My Uncle Marvin was a tall man with ragged, black, shoulder-length hair, and he was drunk too but more in control. Later in life Marvin sobered up and became a source of comfort and inspiration for me.

My life with Gina was fun at times because there were no rules and no school to attend, although she treated me like a live-in babysitter. We moved from her basement apartment into a townhouse in the east end of Edmonton. Gina kept a tidy home and cooked well and my only complaint was the amount of drugs they smoked. Floyd always had hash on him; he would stick it to the bottom of his lighter or in his cigarette package. I can remember him losing his hash and freaking out. Floyd had a loud, booming voice and he literally tore the living room apart looking for his lump of hash. It was about this time they noticed that Cheyenne had a glassy-eyed look. That poor baby had eaten his hash and was stoned but they refused to take her to the hospital. I was sixteen and didn't know any better. Floyd said she would sleep it off, and we believed him.

Gina decided I needed to get drunk so she snuck me into a bar called Truckers, which had a big truck rig in the middle of the dance floor that the DJ played music from. Gina had me all dressed up in high-heeled boots, makeup and sexy clothes, and I kept the drinks to a minimum and had a blast. I guess this was the beginning of my risk-taking behaviour. From there I went to an after-hours bar called the Grasshopper. I had no idea where I was going; I just got in the cab with a guy I had been dancing with. The Grasshopper was loud and black light made anyone who was wearing white pop out. People were snorting white stuff into their noses. Then my memory becomes a blur. I remember going back to this guy's place and kissing for a bit, then he left to go to the bathroom. After waiting about twenty minutes for him to come out, I went into the bathroom and found him passed out on the floor with his leopard-patterned underwear around his ankles. I grabbed the two packs of cigarettes and two twenty-dollar bills from the bedside table and caught a cab home. It was already getting light outside. My sister was up waiting for me, pacing and angry that I hadn't come home after the bar.

Gina and Floyd used to argue a lot. One night Gina hadn't cooked supper by the time Floyd came home from work and he ranted and raved and ended up cooking supper himself. Gina refused to eat it and told me not to eat it either. Floyd freaked out and turned the whole table upside down. Purple Kool-Aid, chicken and rice went flying everywhere. I guess Gina had had enough of her husband's yelling, because she packed a few bags and we caught a cab to her friend Tina's. Floyd showed up after the second day and begged and pleaded for her to come home. We ended up returning to the townhome and he swore that he would change, but he never did.

I was getting restless. I had no friends and was sick of sitting around all day broke or babysitting for Gina. I started venturing downtown to find my family and began visiting with my aunties on my mom's side. At sixteen years I hadn't really developed a fear of people and was curious about everyone and everything. I put myself in a lot of dangerous situations, which I am grateful to have survived to write about today.

I later found out that a lot of people on skid row drank Listerine, Lysol, hairspray, cheap wine and even Chinese cooking wine. My mother was one of those people who hung around skid row, right across from the liquor store in a condemned white house. This house had no heating and no lights and they would drink and use the house as a party place. These parties consisted mostly of my mom's sisters, June, Cece and Roseanne; Marvin; Albert; my *kokum*, Maggie; my mom, Esther; and various other street characters. They would sit around on the broken steps of the condemned house or on broken chairs and drink Lysol mixed with water from a four-quart, emptied-out milk jug. I watched my Uncle Marvin puncture a can of Lysol, drain the contents into a jug and mix it with water. He went from being a quiet, calm man who shared a tea and rolled cigarette with me to a loud, obnoxious, belligerent man who I did not want to be around. My aunties fist-fought with each other, shoved each other and sometimes got into my face because they were too drunk to remember who I was. Thankfully, someone always rescued me because I was "the baby."

I never drank Lysol or anything of that sort with my family. I just watched, observed their behaviours and smoked their cigarettes. I was fascinated with their behaviour, why they drank Lysol and how my mom socialized with her family. It passed the time and I felt like it was the only way I could get to know them.

One day I showed up and my *kokum*, Maggie, was passed out on the sidewalk but no one had noticed because they were so drunk. A passerby must have called the ambulance because within a few minutes a fire truck and an ambulance showed up. *Kokum* Maggie still had not moved and she was a very large woman. I'm guessing she must have exceeded 350 pounds. It took six firemen to put her on a board and lift her onto the stretcher, and my drunken family was trying to intervene by not letting the paramedics and firemen do their job. It was horrible to watch and it was my first humiliating experience on skid row. I was so ashamed of my family. The Edmonton Police arrived and were asking me questions about my *kokum* that I couldn't answer. They were trying to kick everyone out of the house and it was turning into a giant fiasco. I took off to my friend Gordon's house around the corner, and after that day the white house by the liquor store was officially condemned and boarded up.

Gordon lived on 96th Street; he had a little house that he shared with his friend Rick. Gordon sometimes drank at the white house before it was condemned and my Aunty June had introduced me to him. He was twenty-six years old and I would end up moving in with him after getting into a big fight with my sister.

It was June when Gordon and I hooked up. There were constant parties and he took care of me, somewhat. He would cook for me and take me to the laundromat but mostly I sat around waiting for things to happen. He didn't work and neither did anyone else in the house. Back then you could draw a welfare cheque just for being alive and pretending to look for work. I was a pretty naïve girl. One day a bunch of Gordon's friends showed up and they all went upstairs into Rick's room. It was very secretive and I wasn't allowed in the room. I did walk by and noticed someone leaning over a girl and giving her a needle. I had no idea what they were doing; IV drug use was not something I was familiar with. Rick caught me sneaking a peek into his room and said, "Little girl, you don't want none of this," and shut the door on me.

My Aunty June did not like that I was sixteen years old and living with a grown man, so she started threatening to call the police on him for statutory rape. Gordon and his roommate were up to something; they kept talking about taking a trip to Calgary and I was supposed to go with them. The next night, after an evening of drinking, I went to bed sick and very drunk. I woke up to yelling outside my bedroom and found Gordon sitting in the hallway closet, naked, with a loaded rifle. He was crying and going on about killing himself. I was terrified he would do it and tried to take the gun away from him. This was very intense and I couldn't deal with the situation. Another man named Pat, who had been at the party, heard me screaming for help and managed to get the gun away from Gordon and talk him out of killing himself. Later that day Gordon and Rick dropped me off at my sister's place with the understanding that they would come back to get me when we were leaving for Calgary. I stayed up all night and they never came back. It was probably the best thing that could have happened to me; I heard they robbed someone and fled to Calgary. I never saw Gordon again after that.

Back at my sister Gina's place, she was getting ready to move back to 109th Street, the downtown area around Kingsway Mall. After the move I began to wander the streets looking for something to do. I walked all over Chinatown, visited my dad and one of my dad's friends, Virginia. She was an interesting character and always had lots of people at her apartment. I thought she was popular but then I realized she was a user and drug dealer of Ts & Rs (Talwin and Ritalin), a street drug known as "poor man's coke." I caught on one day when Gina and I were visiting along with her daughter Cheyenne, who was about two years old. I watched Gina and Virginia crush some pills and mix them with water, then pull it up into a syringe and proceed to inject themselves with this concoction. Virginia's arms and legs were riddled with bruises and abscesses from missed injection attempts. I was very angry at my sister because up to that point I hadn't known she used IV drugs. I remember saying to her daughter, "Watch and learn, Cheyenne." Gina did not like that comment and told me not to tell Floyd that she shot up.

I have to admit, I was fascinated with the drugs, alcohol and street life culture — if you can call it a culture. Maybe a lifestyle?

I was always watching but never participating in drug activity and almost everyone I knew used drugs in some way, whether it was needles, smoking, snorting or selling. That lifestyle was the norm. I was never scared or afraid of the people who did drugs but I *was* afraid of the drugs themselves. I witnessed people doing "the chicken," a slang term for convulsing from snorting coke or injecting. The stories I heard about people getting beat up, getting guns to the head, being stabbed, having bad trips and overdosing were enough to keep me from using chemical drugs such as cocaine, heroin, pills or acid. I smoked hash with my sister and Floyd occasionally but it made me paranoid and nauseated: not a fun high for me.

In the new apartment downtown, I liked wandering around, going into different stores and pretending I was a tourist experiencing a foreign country for the first time. One day, as I was walking back to my sister's house from an adventure by myself, a nice looking man walking by stopped me and asked what I was doing and struck up a conversation with me on the sidewalk. I was so naïve and trusting. He told me his date had stood him up and asked if I wanted to go for dinner and a beer. He was short, about 5'4", and he was dressed in a shiny suit. He introduced himself as Wayne and we walked the eight blocks to his place in Chinatown. It was just a little bachelor apartment but it was decorated in Chinese fans and pictures on freshly painted blue walls. It was a well-kept place and I was impressed. Wayne changed out of his suit into a more casual outfit and then we continued to walk downtown to a bar called Teddy's on Jasper Avenue. I was sixteen and he was twenty-seven. He had a full-time job customizing vans and seemed to have his shit together. He ordered a BLT sandwich and beer for me, and afterwards we walked back to his place. I moved in the next day. My relationship with Wayne started off with him wining and dining me, buying me perfume, clothes and anything I wanted. But eventually he asked me to get a part-time job to help out, which I obliged because I wanted my own spending money.

It was only a month or so later that I realized Wayne was extremely jealous. He would check on me during the day at the apartment or drop in unannounced from his work as a delivery man. The first time he hit me, we had been arguing and I called him a little fag and ran out the door. Wayne chased me and punched me in the back, which knocked the breath out of me. I struggled with him as he tried to drag me back to the apartment, then I grabbed his face and rubbed it hard against the crushed glass wall of the house we lived in. I scraped up his face pretty bad but I was fighting for my life. He never hit me again after that but there were times he would lock me out or stalk me when I left him. He would follow me down the street in his van like a predator and I always gave in because he would cry on his knees, begging for forgiveness.

It was about this time I discovered I was pregnant, and when I revealed to Wayne that my test was definitely positive he denied that it was his baby. I was devastated because this meant I was going to be raising my baby alone. I didn't want to tell my friends back home that I was a sixteen-year-old pregnant high school dropout. I ended up staying with Wayne during my pregnancy.

By Christmas 1989, both my sisters had been subpoenaed to testify in court for charges against our adoptive father. The court paid for my eldest sister Gina to fly back to Sault Ste. Marie. It was emotionally draining for her and she was so brave. They were successful in court and won their case. Ronald was subsequently charged with three counts of gross indecency and sexual interference and ordered to pay restitution to my sisters in the amount of $15,000 each. He also served time in a North Bay mental health facility. Right after the court hearings,

Dakota ended up moving to Edmonton. She had her son Stevie with her and was pregnant with another child.

Gina, Dakota and I were all pregnant that Christmas of 1989 and we were all back together in Edmonton. It would be the last six months we'd spend together as a family. During the time Dakota and Gina lived in Edmonton, I was working full time at Taco Time as a server/cook. I would get up at 7 a.m. and walk to work for 8 a.m. I never complained because I felt like I had no choice: I needed to work and make money for the baby on the way.

Meanwhile my relationship with Wayne was still abusive but I felt like I needed him so I continued to endure his abuse. Besides, I really didn't know any different at this point in my life; I thought all men were abusive, controlling and jealous. We lived in a bachelor pad in a rooming house that had mostly older men staying in these one-room units with a shared bathroom. Our neighbour's nickname was "Fish" and he bootlegged whiskey and Pilsner beer out of his little apartment. He was friendly and kept to himself, as did the rest of the tenants. I shared the bathroom with these bachelors and would have to use the same tub to bathe in — but only after giving it a vicious scrubbing.

A young couple lived in the basement unit, and one afternoon Wayne had helped the young woman, Lita, carry her groceries down to the basement. Wayne was flirty with women and I was constantly accusing him of trying to sleep with them. That particular day Wayne told me Lita's boyfriend was sleeping on the couch and I didn't think anything else of it until later that night. At about 3 a.m. someone came pounding on our door, yelling and screaming for Wayne to come help them. It was Lita. I jumped out of bed, grabbed the bat to protect myself and proceeded to make my way outside. As I did, a police officer met me and asked why I had a bat, so I explained and he told me to go back to my apartment. By this time the other tenants were up, all with their robes and messy hair, concerned to see cops everywhere and yellow tape blocking the downstairs entrance. I peeked into Lita's basement window to see her partner's feet stiffly pointing upwards at the end of the couch. A few minutes later Lita came out to tell us he was dead; he had overdosed banging Ts & Rs.

This whole process took all night, until the sun came up, and curiosity kept me waiting outside until they brought the body out on a gurney. Lita figured he must have been dead all day while she had gone grocery shopping and then went back out to party with friends, because when she got home, "He was still sleeping." There was a strange sickly smell mixed with Lita's perfume that made me nauseous for days afterwards. The caretaker of the building told me it was the smell of death and they had to use a special chemical to get rid of the smell in the basement of the building. That was my first experience with death and the finality of dying. It frightened me for weeks afterwards. After that incident I refused to go into the basement of the building by myself because I believed it was haunted.

My first training shift at Taco Time started on the morning after this death happened, and when I got to work my stomach was churning from lack of sleep and nausea. They sent me home to rest after hearing what my night had been like. The job was easy, and within weeks I had proven that I could handle responsibility and do many things at once. They promoted me to shift manager, which earned me $6.80 an hour. This was a fortune back in those days when the minimum wage was $4.75! On paydays my sisters would ask me for money to buy diapers and food. Sometimes I resented being the youngest and taking care of my older sisters. Both had men who should have been working. One day I showed up unexpectedly at Gina's place and by-passed the security door. I could hear Floyd arguing with my sister and her yelling, "You ain't buying dope with it!" They were arguing about the money she was asking to borrow from me. This man thought of dope before his kids, which disgusted me, so I threw twenty bucks at him and bought diapers for my niece.

The problems between my sisters and me started after Dakota had given birth to Jacob in March 1990, when Gina accused her of breastfeeding while using drugs and drinking. Gina came to my door and said we needed to take Dakota's kids from her, but I confided to Dakota what Gina was planning. This caused a huge rift between us girls, and the added tension of my abusive partner Wayne banning them from visiting me was too much. Gina despised Wayne and had tried to beat him up when she found out he'd hit me, so since then he had bad-mouthed her like it was her fault instead of his. Things were tense in our family and I feared running into Floyd or Gina in the neighbourhood because we would get into a physical fight or an argument. Gina was tough and street smart, and I knew if I mouthed off to her she would kick my ass. This conflict caused Dakota to move back to Sault Ste. Marie with Stevie and Jacob, who was a mere two months old at this time.

Gina gave birth to Jonah on April 30, 1990, and he was very sick and had to stay in the hospital for a while because he had swallowed meconium during his delivery. I didn't see much of my sister Gina during that time. I kept to myself and worked right up until my thirty-eighth week of pregnancy. I wasn't allowed to work beyond that date for fear I would give birth or be injured at work. I had walked to work five days a week for all of my pregnancy and was used to standing for eight hours at a time. Wayne and I had managed to move into a main-floor apartment of a house. We furnished Naomi's room with a crib and second-hand baby furniture. She already had a full dresser of clothes. I used to shop at a second-hand store called the

GoodWill Store, and I would buy clean sleepers, undershirts and clothes with every pay cheque. We had stocked up on diapers, bottles and every convenience for the baby's arrival. At that time we didn't know if it was a boy or girl. I loved being pregnant and was very lucky not to experience morning sickness. I think the worst experience of my pregnancy was not making it to the bathroom in time and urinating in my pants — apparently pregnant women have to urinate a lot.

I bought a book called *What to Expect When You're Expecting*,[2] and the inner city clinic I went to for prenatal care gave me booklets on healthy eating and nutrition during pregnancy. I thought it was natural to be having a baby, but the nurses doted on me like I was a child, even though I felt like a grownup woman. I had a natural birth with Wayne by my side; labour was hard and painful but I refused to take any drugs for fear that I wouldn't be in control. I began cursing when it came time to push and the nurse told me I didn't need to swear. Naomi was born on July 3, 1990, and from that moment I knew I was meant to be a mother. My natural instincts kicked in and I was in love with my baby. I was up and walking around by that evening. I walked down to the nursery to get Naomi, fed her, and when it came time to change her diaper, I was shocked to see black tar coming out of her bum. I didn't remember reading about this in the book and I panicked and began crying. I thought something was wrong with Naomi but the nurses rushed in and assured me that it was her first bowel movement and quite normal.

Naomi also had a lot of mucous in her lungs and kept vomiting it up; it was distressing to see that much fluid come out of something so small. The nurses used Naomi to demonstrate to the other mothers how to give your baby a bath. I was proud but also in tears, seeing my sweet baby crying her head off from

2 Heidi Murkoff, *What to Expect When You're Expecting* (First Edition) New York: Workman Publications, 1984.

getting a bath. Nothing in the pregnancy books prepares you for how your motherly instincts kick in when your child is crying from sickness, hurt, fear or pain, or in this case, a simple bath. I cannot bear to see my children crying in pain; even their needles as babies brought me to tears.

Finally, after three days, I was released to go home and I was surprised how easily I settled into taking care of my baby. Gina came to my house and begged to see the baby, so I let her in and all the tension and fighting went away. We were both revelling in the fact that I gave birth to a beautiful baby girl and Gina seemed proud of me and happy to be an aunty. I thought that finally things were going to be all right with our family. I imagined our children growing up together, being each other's playmates and having lots of barbecues and picnics.

## CHAPTER 5

# Maayipayowin

I T WAS JULY 25, 1990, and we had planned a big picnic with some of the neighbours to celebrate Naomi's birth. That morning in the paper I noticed a headline reading "Mother of Two Found Dead in Downtown Park," and it showed a body bag being carted away on a stretcher at Beaver Hills House Park on 105<sup>th</sup> Street and Jasper Avenue. I immediately thought, "Oh it's probably a hooker," and I dismissed it from my mind to prepare for the party. There was a big feast and some of Wayne's co-workers brought food and gifts. It was an amazing day and afterwards I cleaned up and made my way back home with Naomi. The phone was ringing and I grabbed it, surprised to hear my dad's voice. I was exuberant with happiness and began talking about the party. My dad cut me off and said, "My girl, that woman they found in the park was your sister."

I don't remember anything after screaming to my dad to "come help me." I was found sitting in the bathtub with the shower going, dishes broken all over the place and a cigarette that had been tucked behind my ear dripping down my face. Poor Naomi had been screaming in her car seat on the floor while I freaked out in anguish over my dead sister. I don't remember what happened but my landlord had come up to see

OHPIKIIHAAKAN-OHPIHMEH

what the commotion was all about and my dad had showed up during my blackout.

Life became surreal; I'd never had anyone close to me die. The whole night I stayed up crying and wondering what had happened to my sister and who had killed her. I kept playing the scene from that morning over and over: me glancing at the paper, seeing the story and forgetting about it. Now I thought to myself, "I was busy planning a party last night, getting up early in the morning while my sister was lying dead in a park." I wondered if she lay there for a long time before she died. Had she suffered? Did she cry and hope someone would save her? Was her last thought about her children? These thoughts tortured me for years. Later the coroner released details that showed Gina had fought back and died from blunt force trauma.

They had no suspects at the time and I had no word from Floyd. I later found out that he had been questioned as a suspect in her murder because he was the last one to see her alive. I don't really remember much; things are patchy at best and parts are blacked out from my memory. My sister Dakota flew in from Sault Ste. Marie and we attended the wake and sat in a receiving line while guests offered their condolences. I did not know most of them, only Gina's friends and some of Floyd's family. Floyd's sister Alex took my hand and Dakota's hand and led us over to the casket. The whole time Alex was crying and saying how beautiful my sister looked and what a great job they did fixing her up. I had never viewed a dead body in my life and I was terrified. I tried to pull back but Alex forced me to view Gina's battered and bruised body. Dakota was horrified and began screaming and wailing, and I was in shock because the body lying in the casket did not look like my sister, it looked like a monster. Gina's face was flat and deformed from the beating, she had faint bruising under the mortuary makeup and the only thing recognizable was her beautiful long curly hair and hands clasped together on her chest. My poor sister had suffered and it showed. I don't think the casket should have been open because it was not how I wanted to remember her and that last glimpse of her remained with me for a long time. Images of dead, battered Gina haunted my dreams and traumatized me for years afterwards.

Those few days before the funeral were hazy and dream-like. I was going back and forth from the police station, talking with detectives, fielding phone calls from the media and taking care of my one-month-old baby. Floyd's family took care of the preparations for the funeral. I had no support from my boyfriend Wayne; in fact he seemed pleased Gina was dead. The day of the funeral came and since I had never been to a funeral, I didn't know what to expect. Floyd's family had arranged a limo for my sister and me, Floyd's parents and Floyd's sisters and it felt very unreal and fake to be riding in a limo to a funeral.

I could not believe my sister was dead; I could not wrap my head around the fact that she would never walk or talk again. I could not imagine that this meant forever. That feeling took a long time to go away. It was years before I came to accept that my sister would never come back. Grief has no timeline; it sat in my throat, left me on the verge of tears, and my words became bitter and angry. I felt like I was suspended in time. Outside of the church, I hung back a bit, still feeling like things were not real, like it had to be a dream. I watched the hearse pull up to the steps of the church and park, and then they took out the casket and carried it up the stairs to a waiting trolley. I followed slowly behind as my sister's body was wheeled down the church aisle to the front where the priest was waiting. I never looked up or met anyone's stares; the casket was my only focus. Someone was playing church hymns on an organ, women were wailing and people patted my back, but the whole thing felt like an out-of-body experience. "This can't be real," I kept saying to myself. "This can't be real. This is not real."

At the end of the service the funeral director was supposed to play "Thank You" by Led Zeppelin as Gina was wheeled out to the waiting hearse. Instead they mistakenly played "Ramble On," which caused Floyd to loudly bellow that they'd fucked up the funeral. It was an inappropriate, giggly kind of moment and very brief. As her casket reached the doorway of the church, Floyd flung himself onto it and cried for her not to leave. He had to be pried off. I couldn't bear to see him cry.

Gina was buried in a beautiful light-pink casket with silver handles, wearing all her gold jewellery and gold pieces that Floyd's family had donated. Floyd had a large Portuguese family and there seemed to be hundreds of his family members at the service. The Portuguese women, dressed in black veils, were wailing. Our biological mother, Esther, showed up drunk and falling all over the place. As the graveside service began, Esther started grabbing Dakota's arm, trying to see inside the grave. I don't know why she was doing this but I pushed her away from Dakota, who was crying and upset. When I pushed her, my mother lost her footing and almost fell into the grave because she was so drunk. Floyd's brother Manny grabbed her arm and steadied her. It was embarrassing but I was so angry and ashamed that she couldn't even show up sober for my sister's — her daughter's — funeral. I thought it was disrespectful at the time and I was embarrassed that she was my family member. I regret my harsh actions now and accept that Esther did not know any other way to be; losing her firstborn child must have been overwhelming. Later on, after I did some healing, I was able to forgive her for showing up drunk.

As Gina was lowered into her final resting place, her husband Floyd played Led Zeppelin's "Thank You" on a boombox someone had brought to the graveyard. I had never heard it before that day but it felt like it had been written for Gina and me. The lyrics describe the powerful love between two people and the strength it gives them to carry on, no matter what. The song haunted me for a long time and I used to cry every time I heard it because it brought me right back to that day. Now the lyrics make me smile. They remind me of my sister, who continues to inspire me and help to keep me motivated in my ongoing healing work. As hard as life gets, I know Gina wouldn't want me to give up. Sometimes a tear escapes because my body still remembers the grief.

~ ~ ~

Gina, February 2, 1970–July 25, 1990

Those were very hard times for the whole family. In Edmonton we began to realize how significant the loss was to our family. Gina was the glue that kept us together even when we had our differences. She left behind her infant son Jonah, who was four months old at the time, and Cheyenne, who was two years old. She had been a loving mother; those children clung to her, she cuddled them, she played with them every second of the day and I never saw her get weary or tired of taking care of them. She revelled in her role as a mother and I never once heard her raise her voice in anger at her children. She was very protective of them and was their primary caregiver. Her husband Floyd did not change diapers or participate much in the parenting role; if anything, Floyd was the one who was frustrated by the children. But now Floyd was a widowed father of two children he barely knew how to take care of, two children whose mother had been their world.

Later that week, after the funeral, we were notified that the police had caught the man they thought had killed Gina. His name was Scott Jason Atkinson and he was an acquaintance of Floyd and Gina. He used to smoke up with them occasionally and score dope for them. When they caught Atkinson, he was in Calgary and had beat up another woman, leaving her in a coma. He told police that he "killed some bitch up in Edmonton." The details of the trial are murky, but in 1992 he was convicted of second-degree murder and sentenced to thirteen years without parole. It was a difficult time because I was pregnant with Cree; I tried to attend most of the trial but couldn't handle it when they showed the jurors pictures of my sister's battered body.

I was too caught up in my own grief and parenting of Naomi, who was one month old at this time, to help Floyd with my sister's kids. In my own relationship, which was already toxic and emotionally abusive before Gina passed, Wayne had made a comment about being glad Gina was dead. I was shocked at that, but he continued, "How do you know that I didn't do it?"

I left him the next day to live in a woman's shelter. I know he didn't kill my sister but the fact that he made such a comment made me see how much of an asshole he really was. Wayne would sometimes lock me out of the house for the whole day, forcing me to stay with the neighbours while he was at work. That day I decided to leave because it was my best chance at getting away without Wayne being suspicious. The only belongings I had were a bottle for Naomi, a blanket, one can of formula and two sleepers. I had Naomi in a baby carrier on my chest and I took a bus downtown to a crisis welfare office. They put us up in a hotel for one night and gave me a voucher for formula, diapers and some food. I had no idea what the future held for us. After a few days they moved Naomi and me to a new big family shelter in the downtown core area of Edmonton.

At the shelter, everyone had to share rooms with each other's families and cook and eat together. I only stayed there a few nights because Wayne stalked me and they had to move me to another shelter to protect me and everyone else. The added stress of putting other families at risk made me decide to go stay a few days with Lori and Tim, who were former neighbours and friends of mine. They partied a lot and went to bars, and I found this lifestyle fun and an escape from everything else that was going on. I was also quite promiscuous during this time and slept with any man who gave me a little bit of attention. I didn't realize that I was being used by these people and taken advantage of for my welfare cheque. Once Wayne found out I was staying with Lori and Tim, he began to hang around their house at night, stalking me, peeking into their windows. Eventually the police were called and I had to leave because Lori and Tim didn't want to become involved with the police or with Wayne.

The police placed me in another shelter away from the downtown core but Wayne relentlessly stalked me, going everywhere he thought I might be. Little did I know that he already knew where some of the women's shelters were and would sit outside in the van waiting for a glimpse of me or to catch me alone. I would discover later that Wayne had previously stalked and harassed all his ex-girlfriends until they charged him or he moved onto a new woman. One day I was walking back to the shelter and he began driving the van slowly down the street beside me. I ducked into an arcade shop and had them call the shelter, where staff then called the police. I was seventeen years old with a two-month old baby, homeless and living in shelters. It was then that I began to suffer from anxiety, which I had mistaken for hunger. I remember waking up one night in a panic and thinking I must be hungry, so the relief worker on night shift made me tomato soup and crackers at four in the morning. Although that feeling did not go away, I began using food as a consolation for anxiety throughout my adulthood.

The shelter was pushing for me to find my own place because they had a limit on how long you are allowed to stay. Images of my late sister kept me from sleeping; when I closed my eyes I would see her dead body and imagine her death scenario. The shelter was suffocating with so many rules, and sharing my space with other women and children was hard. The women were so mean to each other and unsupportive. I would watch these women's behaviours, their eye and body language towards each other and their children, and it scared me enough that I decided to leave the shelter.

My search for an apartment was gruelling because no one wanted to rent to a young, single mom on welfare. I would later learn that being Indigenous meant people were going to judge me based on my skin colour. I was oblivious to racism and discrimination, or maybe I was just naïve because I was raised white. I would forget that I was Indigenous sometimes. How can you forget that you are Indigenous? Assimilation helps you forget. The fact that someone will treat you different because of your skin colour boggles my mind to this day.

I was able to find a small one-room bachelor apartment for Naomi and me but it was terrifying to be all alone and cut off from the world. I had no phone, no television, and I felt very alone taking care of Naomi while still grieving the loss of my sister Gina. No family or friends visited me and I began wishing a man would come and rescue me from the horrible life I was living. After all these years, I now realize that I didn't want any man to rescue me — I wanted a dad, a father to rescue me and show me the love, kindness and tenderness that I had never known. To this day I am still waiting, although I am aware it will never happen until I resolve that need. I'm learning, and writing about it helps.

Tim and Lori had come up with a plan to move me into their townhouse under the guise of helping me. Little did I know that they needed my welfare cheque to supplement the rent for their new house. I jumped at the opportunity to move in with them because I was so lonely. Naomi and I had a bedroom in the basement, and though it was all right most of the time because it was a beautiful house, I didn't feel part of the household. During Christmas I didn't spend any time in the house but went to spend Christmas with my dad's friend Pauline. She was an older lady in her late thirties and had invited Naomi and me over for dinner. She was also greasing the wheels to get on my dad's good side because she had a crush on him. Her efforts were in vain; my dad couldn't have cared less about her and told me she was a drunken loudmouth.

It was during that Christmas dinner that I met my third abuser, the most violent of them all: Charles. He was tall, with black hair in a long mullet, which was fashionable at that time for men. He was wearing skin-tight Levi jeans and an Oilers hockey jersey. He was so handsome and he was staring at me! What I didn't know at that time was that he had just done a B&E (break and enter) and was driving a stolen truck. He had a gold necklace that he put on my neck, then he had a few beers with us and left. The next day he showed up again and we began drinking. It was a whirlwind few days of drinking and having sex, and then it was time to leave. I took Charles home with me, along with his duffel bag of belongings. I don't know what I was thinking but in the space of three or four short days, I was in love and in a relationship.

New Year's Eve arrived and Charles went out to meet his brothers and friends. He came back around 10 p.m., drunk and high on a concoction of pills. He could not walk properly and fell into the snow-covered flowerbeds as he stumbled up the front walkway. His eyes looked glassy as he stared off into somewhere unseen. Even as he looked at me, it was like he wasn't seeing me. I'll remember that look for the rest of my life; it was the same one he had after he almost killed me during another drunken rage. Charles and his brother Jermaine walked into the townhouse I shared with Tim and Lori and began poking into cupboards, looking for valuables to steal or pills to take. They were so brazen and terrifying at the same time. I was horrified because Lori and Tim were pissed off that these strangers were so drunk and high in their house. I demanded Charles leave. Later that night he was arrested, charged with grand theft auto and sentenced to six months in Grande Cache jail. I was very embarrassed that he had shown up so intoxicated at my roommates' house. He reminded me of the Indigenous people you see pilled up and stumbling around on skid row.

Problems began with Lori and Tim as soon as I started working part-time at Taco Time again and leaving Naomi in their care. One day after work, I came home to find Naomi screaming, in a very soaked diaper. She was dripping with sweat and had been left in the basement in my room, possibly for hours. Furious at them for neglecting my daughter, I packed up what I could and left.

I was homeless once again so I moved in with my dad Ricky, but there was hardly any room for Naomi and me. Things were grim during that time and my dad fell off the wagon for a few days, something I had never seen him do. He had been working (and succeeding) at staying sober for a while, but I think the death of Gina really impacted him. I had to take care of him and make sure he ate and slept. At his worst moment during his relapse, he flew into a rage, pushing me and accusing me of stealing the beer he'd previously hidden in his closet and forgotten about. I was terrified he would hit me. Eventually

Ricky sobered up and never drank again — or at least I never saw him drunk again during the twelve years that I lived in Edmonton.

My temptation to go back to Wayne was strong, and one day I left Naomi at home and ventured downtown with a hunting knife. I didn't intend to hurt anyone but since Gina had died, I felt I needed protection. My dad gave me the knife and I would carry it everywhere with me. I showed up at Wayne's place downtown to talk and saw his new girlfriend, Geraldine, through the window. I brought my knife out and began banging on the door, yelling that I had a knife. What was I thinking? I just wanted to scare her and it worked; she left Wayne later and I was able to convince him to move back with me.

Wayne and I got a new apartment close to my father's place and things settled back into the status quo. Wayne had not changed, I had just lowered my standards to secure a father for my child and because I was scared to be alone. Wayne would pester me and antagonize me, literally harassing me in the apartment. If I tried to sleep, he would stand over me until I answered his questions. Whether I was right or wrong, it didn't matter because there was no right answer, only more questions like "How many men did you sleep with?" "Were they better lovers?" or "Why do you hurt me so much?" The questions were never-ending. I would end up lashing out at him because I was so frustrated and felt trapped. My father did not like Wayne. One day he insulted my dad's bannock, saying "Eww, what is that?" My father grabbed him by his collar and put him up against the fridge, telling him "I don't fuckin' like you, don't fuck with me," then pushed him away. I started laughing at Wayne and he took off out of the apartment right away, mad at me for not leaving with him. I told him, "Don't mess with me or my dad will kick your butt."

One evening I managed to go out to with my neighbour

Penny. I can't remember how we ended up at the bar but I began telling some men there how Wayne treated me. These men came back to the apartment with Penny and me and roughed Wayne up a bit by punching him and warning him not to mess with me. Why did I let them do this? Why did I allow this to happen? I don't know, maybe I was feeling vengeful and wanted to pay Wayne back for saying he was the one who killed my sister.

In June of 1991, I was inquiring into receiving my Indian status card at Indian and Northern Affairs Canada (INAC) when I was informed that a cheque for $39,000 had been mailed to my previous address at Lori and Tim's. INAC had held my money in trust from oil royalties, and when I turned eighteen, I was able to collect them! What are the chances that I would call the day that cheque was mailed out?

My neighbour Penny drove me over to my former address to wait for the mailman. I intercepted him at the door and showed him my photo ID health card. He handed over the cheque and we headed to the bank. I could not cash the cheque because I didn't have federal government identification so I took it home and hid it in a cereal box in the cupboard. I didn't tell Wayne about the money. First thing the next morning, Penny drove me to Indian and Northern Affairs on Jasper Avenue, where they took my picture and gave me an ID card on the spot. We headed to the bank and I deposited $39,000 into my account, and the bank manager came over and shook my hand. I didn't heed the bank representative's advice to put money into a GIC. I immediately withdrew $1,500, which was the most I could take out in one day. I went home and promptly told Wayne he could move out. It was during this conversation that I heard a familiar voice outside the balcony. I ran out to see Charles and his brother Jermaine standing outside waiting for me. I ran outside into the lobby and was greeted by Charles — he hugged me and lifted me off the floor. I had forgotten that I wrote him a letter while he was incarcerated, giving him my address and telling him to come see me when he got out. Oh yes, he came to see me in a stolen car with a broken windshield. I didn't find out it was stolen 'til months later, after I'd paid $250 to get the windshield fixed! My boyfriend situation was a mess at that time because I was trying to get Wayne out of the apartment and still see Charles, who was huge and muscular from lifting weights in jail. Charles threatened Wayne that if he didn't get out, he would make him get out. I thought this was pretty cool at the time and I liked that my boyfriend was tough and stood up for me. Now that I am writing it out, though, it sounds pretty horrible.

We partied hard that night, drinking and eating pizza. I had money to spend! Oh, if I'd had the foresight to see how many people would take advantage of my money. I admit I gave my dad and my brother Lucky about $6,000. My dad bought an old broken-down trailer and Lucky bought lots of clothes. Charles and I bought matching fringe leather jackets. I even gave money to Charles's brother to buy new clothes. I paid the tab for all the beer, food and clothes. Everyone partied on my dime. I bought black couches, marble end tables, a huge thirty-two-inch TV and a customized candy-blue low-rider Chevy truck. Charles and I did not have licences so my dad put the insurance in his name. Charles drove most of the time and he took a lot of chances, driving fast and even driving drunk.

The money was starting to run low and we got evicted from my apartment after neighbours complained about all the noise and drinking. It was heading into August and I was down to my last $900. This is when my relationship started to go bad and turn abusive. One day we were outside and Charles had sworn at Naomi and I slapped his face. He immediately slapped my face back, hard. I was shocked and angry that he hit me.

Within weeks my life began a terrifying turn and Charles

started to show his true colours. The first time I saw his propensity for violence was when we drank some whiskey. He began wrestling me and playing around, but then he hit me hard in the head with the whiskey bottle. I shook it off as horseplay. A few days later, his brothers Jermaine and Carmen and I went to the bar to drink and wait for Charles to show up. He arrived about an hour later and he was mad that his brothers were drinking with me. I didn't realize at this time how violently jealous he was if any man looked at me or talked to me. On our way back to the house, Charles staged a coup against Carmen and Jermaine. They began to fight and punch each other. The brothers attacked Charles and at one point he scraped his back on the grill of the truck. He was bleeding a lot but he kept on fighting his brothers. At one point I was in the house and Jermaine and Carmen would not let me off the patio. Charles was standing on the front lawn demanding that I come out to him. Jermaine blocked my path and said to me, "This guy is not for you, he has done everything that you can imagine except for rape and murder."

I should have heeded Jermaine's warning but I dared not take sides against Charles. The brothers left, but later that night Jermaine came back and broke into the basement of our house. Charles hurt him real bad. He dropped a tire on his head and stabbed him in the head with a broken broom handle. It was a very violent fight and I thought Charles was trying to kill Jermaine. I hid in the closet, clutching Naomi to my chest. After a few minutes I ventured out of the closet, fearful of finding someone dead or dying. Charles had chased Jermaine out of the house and down the street. I sat on the porch waiting for him to return and within a few minutes we also saw Jermaine come back up the sidewalk. He had his head bowed and he got down on his knees in front of Charles and gave up a stick he was using as a weapon. It was the strangest thing I had ever seen. Jermaine was afraid of Charles and he knew it. This was my first clue then that Charles was a monster but I still liked that he was tough and dangerous — I was in deep with him.

The next time, his anger was directed at me. My father Ricky and little brother Lucky had moved into the basement to help us pay the rent. The house was a shitbox and the rugs smelled of mould but I didn't care at the time because we needed a place to live after being evicted. My father and Charles did not like each other, and more than once my father threatened to take the insurance off the truck because Charles was irresponsible. On this occasion, Charles had gone out for the day and ended up drinking with one of my father's ex-girlfriends, a woman named Virg. He went to a party and was drinking whiskey and the people there ganged up on him. He came back very drunk and angry, yelling at me and blaming my father for getting those people to beat him up. Charles smashed the table to bits with his fists and became angrier by the minute. At one point he was in my face yelling; he put a knife to my chest and I felt the tip of the blade go into the skin between my breasts. My father and Lucky were out for the evening, and thank god, because Charles was planning on stabbing him or beating him up. Charles was yelling around the house, searching the basement and threatening to harm my father. My heart was frozen with fear. I could hear him yelling in the basement that my father had stabbed him, then he came up the stairs with a knife lodged in his leg. He ordered me to pack up Naomi and get into the truck, saying he wanted to drive up North to see his uncle. I was terrified that Charles would try to stab me, so we piled into the truck and didn't even make it one block before he almost hit a pedestrian.

Within minutes I heard sirens and we were pulled over. The police approached with their guns drawn and ordered us out of the truck. The knife was still stuck in Charles's leg and he was bleeding. The police were asking me questions about what was going on and Charles looked at me and said, "Don't you dare tell them my name!" But I did. Charles was immediately arrested and the truck left by the side of the road. I was taken into the police station for questioning and they took photos of the wound in my chest. Charles had cut the skin but not deep enough to require stitches. Afterwards the police brought me home and examined the damage in the house. One of the police officers drove my truck home. Charles was charged with assaulting me with a weapon and drunk driving. This time he got four months' incarceration. I never even considered that I should break up with him. I was a loyal punching bag.

I was now broke, evicted, with a damaged truck full of blood on the driver's side. I paid $8,000 for that truck and ended up selling it for $1,500. My sister Dakota's ex-boyfriend Sam decided to move to Edmonton with his new girlfriend, Tamara. Sam had Dakota's kid Stevie in his care while her other son, Jacob, was being raised by my father Ricky. I can't recall where Ricky went after these events; I believe he moved out to Onihcikiskowapowin (Saddle Lake Cree Nation) for a while with my brother Richard and Jacob. I moved in with Sam and Tamara and things went from bad to worse. Sam was just as abusive to Tamara and his son Stevie as Charles was to me. They smoked pot in their bedroom and he would smack Tamara or pull her hair when he abused her. He was mean to Stevie and would freak out if he pooped in his diaper or didn't use the potty. It was horrible but I put up with it because I needed a place to stay. Calling Child Services on him was never a consideration; I just minded my own business.

Life was horrible — Dakota had abandoned her kids after Gina died and was living on the streets of Edmonton, partying, drugging and prostituting to support her lifestyle. She was hurting so bad. My dad had left the city and I had virtually no one to rely on for support. I remember we went to the food bank a lot and lived on "No Name" Kraft dinner, hot dogs and soup. We smoked butts, pawned off the rest of my belongings, and I settled in for a long, depressing winter.

Charles was released on an early day program so he would come home for the day under the guise of looking for work. He would spend the day with me and then go back to the jail for the evening. He promised to make it up to me and get me out of Sam's household, because Sam was now the villain, not Charles. Eventually Charles was released and we moved into another apartment and applied for welfare. That first Christmas together was bleak; I could barely afford to buy Naomi any presents. She was only two years old at the time though, and I guess you don't need too many presents when you're that young.

It was about this time my Aunty Lisa on my mother's side decided to take an interest in my existence. She had been sober for a long time and had her own kids with her *môniy'w* (white man) husband, Bob. She would give me second-hand clothes for Naomi, invite me to dinner and sometimes babysit Naomi. She fed us Christmas dinner and it was my first real Christmas meal in the four years since I'd left Sault Ste. Marie. This was the closest thing I had to family at that time in my life. Floyd moved close to where we lived so I was able to see Gina's kids often and I always babysat them. The problem started when Floyd began to leave the kids with me all the time and not return for days. I resented being the caregiver all the time. He would never pay me despite always promising money in his conniving way. I felt obligated to take care of my late sister's kids, a feeling I had come to despise over the course of my life: obligation.

I became pregnant with Cree in December 1991. During that time it was tolerable living with Charles, though one night he got drunk, broke into someone's truck and stole a large car jack. He came home with it at 4 a.m., dragging it up three flights of stairs. Bang! Bang! Bang! I could hear the tire jack hitting each stair as he dragged it up to our apartment. I was sure someone would call the police but no one did.

Charles's sister Linda came to stay with us for a while because she was fleeing abuse from her partner in Hobbema. Linda brought her children and one of them had cerebral palsy. She would have to massage the girl's limbs and constantly work them to keep them from going stiff. Linda was sweet; she had a soft voice and looked like a pretty version of her brother, with the same naturally curly hair. It was then that I learned of Charles's background, which no one else had told me about. One evening over coffee while Charles was out, Linda told me about her family and siblings.

Charles was the oldest of five siblings. His father, Royce, worked on the trap line and would be gone for weeks. When he came off the trap line he would drink and beat his wife, Charles's mother, Brenda. Linda told me that her father was also jealous and one night he was so drunk he killed his wife. Charles got all of his siblings out of the cabin and ran into the woods with them. A few days later, I asked Charles to tell me this story of his life. He told me almost the same story but he also said that his father cut off his mother's hands and shot her. Charles said his father tried to shoot him as he ran away with the kids. Royce spent time in jail for murdering his wife, and the day after he was released someone in Charles's mother's family shot him in the head. I really felt sorry for Charles at that point. He talked about growing up in foster care and being split up from his siblings. It sounded really messed up and very tragic — but little did I know that telling the story might have triggered something in Charles.

Linda eventually found an apartment and moved out on her own. I didn't see her after that at all. I did hear that she partied a lot and eventually gave the kids back to the father in Hobbema. In 2004 she was reported missing. Her remains were found in a coulee just outside of Wetaskiwin. Her death was deemed suspicious but there were no suspects. To this day the case remains unsolved, another one of the many unsolved murders of Indigenous women in and around the Edmonton area.

One day during the summer of 1992, while I was pregnant, Charles went out with a few cousins of his. He left and told me he was going to borrow $50 from his cousin. He stayed out all night and returned home the next afternoon with hickeys all over his neck. He claimed his cousin Dawn had pranked him while he was passed out but he also had scratches on his back — we call those "fuck marks." I never believed him and knew he had cheated on me with his cousin. It later came out that they'd had an ongoing affair for years. Even his cousin Paula told me she knew about it, and I was disgusted that his father's family all talked about Charles as if he were a horse who was sowing his wild oats. No one saw anything wrong with cousins sleeping together in his family. Later on Charles would have a relationship with Dawn and live with her for a summer.

Cree was born September 2, 1992. I was the proud mother of a son and Charles was there with me through the whole labour and delivery. We brought our baby son home and Naomi doted on her little brother. Charles was helpful most of the time, too. He was a proud dad and took his turn changing diapers and feeding the baby. I had decided to go back to work part-time and left the kids alone with Charles. I had only worked for two days when I came home to a very quiet Naomi, which was not like her. Later that night I was giving her a bath and noticed a very large bruise in the shape of a hand on her butt. I began crying because I knew Charles must have hit her very hard to leave a bruise that big. I quickly dressed Naomi and made an excuse that I was going to see Floyd to get a couple of smokes. I ran over to Floyd's apartment and showed him the bruises. He wanted to kick the crap out of Charles but we called the police instead. Charles was arrested that evening and charged with assault. He only got three months and was released early, after one month.

During that time I took in a roommate named Nicole and we partied a little bit while Charles was in jail. A few times I had a few people over and we drank. A neighbour told Charles that after he was released I had men in my apartment and was partying. Charles confronted me and I told him that, yes, I did have a few people over but nothing happened. The issue was not brought up again but a week later we decided to hit the bar and everyone was in good spirits. Charles, Nicole, Jermaine and I went to a bar called Truckers. Everyone was happy and there was no indication that anything was going to happen that night. I was sitting at the bar table with Nicole and some other people I knew, and Charles had gone to the bathroom. Somehow I knocked over a bottle with my elbow and it fell to the floor. Just as that happened, a man walking by said jokingly, "You're cut off," meaning I should stop drinking. We both laughed, but Charles saw this exchange from across the bar and assumed I was cheating on him. He came over and started roughing up the poor guy, who had no idea what was happening. Six bouncers escorted Charles out of the bar. I knew I was in trouble and Nicole and I jumped in a cab as quickly as we could. I ended up beating Charles home, paid the babysitter and then locked the door. I heard Charles and Jermaine outside the door, arguing. They began fighting and I could hear Jermaine screaming in pain. I later learned Charles had tried to press his fingers into Jermaine's eyes.

Within minutes I heard a knock on the door. It was Charles and he was saying, "Baby, let me in, it's okay, I'm all right." A huge rush of relief went through me. I unlocked the door, and the next thing I knew I was flying through the air into the closet. Charles had punched me right in the face and sent me flying.

While I was down, he began to kick me all over: in my breasts, my legs, anywhere that he could kick. I was so disoriented and shocked from the pain of the punch that I could not get back up. He would not stop kicking me. Nicole jumped in and he began to beat her also. I guess she figured he wouldn't hit her but she was mistaken. We tried to escape out the door but he grabbed our hair and dragged us down the hallway to the apartment as we screamed for someone to help us. Not one person helped us or opened their door, though I don't blame them; he probably would have beaten them up, too. I was in such a state of fear as I tried to escape that I never even considered I would be leaving my children alone in that apartment with him.

The beating went on for another half-hour at least. He chased us into the bathroom with a knife and the only thing that stopped him from stabbing us was the knife getting stuck in the door. He was trying to force his way in the bathroom while we were pushing as hard as we could to keep the door shut, and finally it came right off the hinges. I remember pissing and shitting my pants in fear — shit and piss literally ran down my legs because I had no control over what my body was doing.

Nicole and I were covered in blood as we fought for our lives. Charles dragged us to the living room and made us sit on the couch. He put the telephone on my lap and said, "Call the cops, I fuckin' dare you," and then he whacked my hands with a steel pipe when I tried to dial. The steel pipe he had was from the baby swing that he had dismantled and was using to beat us. He hit Nicole across the front of the head with the pipe and blood started running down her face, and then he smacked me in the back of the head with the pipe and split my scalp open. I could feel blood streaming down my back. I blacked out for a short time, but what brought me out of it was hearing my children screaming their heads off in the bedroom. I was so afraid he would harm them because they were crying. Nicole was still bleeding badly down her face and Charles ordered her to go to the washroom and clean up. It was then that she escaped out a bedroom window and called the police. Charles still had me sitting on the couch, yelling at me that he was "Royce," his late father. His eyes had that glassy look like he wasn't seeing me, but there was also something demonic in that stare. I recall that with shivers, even as I write this.

It might have been five or ten minutes before Charles noticed Nicole was not in the bathroom. He told me I'd better find her; he actually thought she was hiding. I pretended to look in the bedroom, the cupboards, anything to distract Charles for a few minutes so Nicole would have time to get away. He turned his fury on me when he realized she had escaped. He ordered me to wash up the blood on my face and to change my clothes. As I was changing I remembered there was $900 in cash in my pocket, so I pushed it under the mattress just in case he decided to take it from me. When I stood up he punched me so hard that I flew across the bed and into the closet. I was dazed for a minute and then all of a sudden men were jumping through the windows and they had Charles at gunpoint against the wall. A tactical team had stormed our basement apartment and there were cops everywhere. I grabbed my kids out of the crib and I remember the police pulling me out of the bedroom and questioning me about what had happened. They asked if Charles had done this to me, and I could hear him telling the police that someone had broken into the apartment and beat us up. Charles then looked at me and said "Six months is nothing compared to what I'll do to you when I get out!"

The officer questioning me was distracted trying to get Charles in cuffs and I took the opportunity to run with my kids. I thought the police would believe his story and he would be released. I ran to the opposite end of the building and hid in the stairwell. I was bleeding all over Cree's head as I held him close to my body. He was only three months old. Naomi was crying from fear. I was trying to keep them quiet but my body was severely traumatized and shocked and I couldn't stop shaking from fear. All I could picture was Charles finding me and killing me.

Blackness took over for a minute. I struggled to stay alert as the grey walls of unconsciousness were closing in on me. Maybe it was from loss of blood or from being hit so much but I was not in good shape. The police were looking for me and I could hear them calling my name down the hallways. Eventually they found me cowering in the stairwell. They took my kids and held them while the paramedics treated me. The police assured me that Charles would be going to jail for a long time. As we walked to the ambulance, we passed the cruiser that Charles was in and I saw him watching me — you cannot fathom the terror I felt as I walked by. I was sure he would be released or break out of the squad car.

While the paramedics were treating me in the lobby of the apartment, surrounded by neighbours all wondering what was happening, one of the paramedics made a snarky remark to one of the young Indigenous women standing by: "This is what happens when you drink." This made my blood boil and I angrily asked, "You think I deserve to be beat up because I had a few beers?"

Jermaine had returned and offered to take care of the kids while I went to the hospital. Nicole and I were treated for our wounds and a chart with a drawing of a little figure was brought out to document the many cuts, bruises, contusions and injuries I had. The nurse was kind and gentle as I cried in humiliation and pain. They counted fifty-two injuries to my body including: two black eyes, swollen cheeks and split lips; painfully hard contusions on both of my breasts, thighs, hands and forearms; and all my fingers were green, purple and black with bruises, though there were no broken bones. The nurse had to examine each bruise and contusion, feeling for swelling and checking for breaks. I had a concussion and needed five stitches in the back of my head. My jaw also felt dislocated. Chewing would prove to be difficult for a few months. I had lost some tissue on my shin and I had globs of blood dried into my scalp and blood crusted to my head and hair. I was in so much pain that they prescribed me Tylenol 3s, then sent me home.

I came back to a bloody, messy house and found Jermaine passed out with a kid in the crooks of both arms. Nicole and I slept together that morning, traumatized, hugging each other till we fell asleep.

I called my dad Ricky the next day and was met with no sympathy. In fact, he basically told me that everyone knew Charles would beat me up sooner or later. I had relatives on my dad's side living in an apartment block close to ours and they had heard about the assault and were talking about it like hot gossip. Nicole and I had a big mess to clean up. There were broken ashtrays and glass everywhere, blood on the walls and sheets, drops of blood on the rugs and a knife stuck in a door off the hinges. A solemn hopeless atmosphere hung with the stale cigarette smell. I think I was in robot mode because I just went through the motions of cleaning, taking care of the children and getting through the day.

Charles called in the afternoon the day after; he was asking why he was in jail and what had happened. I was in disbelief that he could not remember that he'd almost killed us. I told him not to call me again, and for a while I did not hear from him. I was grieving the loss of the relationship but by this time you're probably wondering why the hell I would be grieving and missing the man after everything he had done to me. I now know that I didn't love him; I was co-dependent on him.

## CHAPTER 6

# Paspiiwin

NICOLE AND I DECIDED to move to another apartment because I didn't feel safe in the basement suite anymore. I was having nightmares and couldn't sleep. I started to drink heavily to cope with the anxiety and trauma I had experienced. I was also having dizzy spells from the concussions, problems eating because I couldn't swallow, and it felt like I had something blocking my throat — I think it was anxiety. We had lots of house parties and I was oblivious to my kids. I don't remember much about that time except that I was drinking excessively in the weeks after my assault. Charles was sentenced to eighteen months in prison for two counts of aggravated assault against Nicole and me. He started doing his time at the Fort Saskatchewan Correctional Centre and was later transferred to the Drumheller Institution, a medium security prison near Calgary.

When Nicole and I moved into the new place we continued to throw parties and I ended up meeting Joseph, the father of my third child, Carla Charmaine. Dakota came over one night and we were drinking with her boyfriend Robert, who had a knobby red nose from drinking too much wine. He looked like a troll and was not attractive at all. Robert had brought another man with him, Joseph, who was handsome and had long black hair. At first he seemed like a jerk. He barely spoke but after a few beers we started talking about both being Scorpios and things we had in common. It wasn't too long before we were kissing and heading to the bedroom. I remember Joseph telling me how "deadly" he was in bed but we never did get to that point because we both passed out drunk.

I woke up with a stranger; I couldn't remember his name but he was leaning over the crib giving Cree a bottle. We were both shy and it was an awkward moment because he couldn't remember my name either, but we both liked each other and decided to see each other again. We fell into a relationship from that day onwards and only later would I find out that Joseph was on the run from a Canada-wide warrant for arson. While I was getting to know Joseph there were warning signs that he was not exactly "good" boyfriend material. I mean, he knew how to cook, clean and help out around the house but he was a binge drinker and would take off whenever he felt the need to drink. At least once a week he would be gone all night.

Christmas came and went quickly and I barely managed to pull it off. I did some last-minute shopping by dipping into the rent money. By January 1, 1993, I had spent all the rent money on booze, food and cigarettes. The landlord was a young woman, and when she came to collect I remember her saying, "I thought you were different, Colleen." She was referring to the crazy party animal I had become and not the charming chameleon I had presented to her in order to get the apartment.

January, February and March rolled by as Dakota and I enrolled in a course called FLIP, an acronym for Family Life Improvement Program. It was a ten-week course, with daycare provided, for young mothers to improve parenting skills and gain self-confidence. I was on welfare and it required me to attend workshops, practice résumé writing or do something productive to try and get back into the workforce. I completed the course but was pregnant again and expecting in December

1993. I was evicted from the building on 66<sup>th</sup> Street and Joseph and I scrambled to find a place to live.

During this time I was learning more about Joseph and discovered he was an IV drug user, shooting up coke whenever he could find it. I was so naïve, I didn't even know until my brother-in-law Floyd called him out on it in front of me. He told Joseph, "You better tell Colleen what the holes in your arm are about." Floyd knew about it because he used drugs also. But I didn't even care. I was so preoccupied with finding a new place, coping with two young children, and surviving on food bank donations that I was grateful for the child care and emotional support Joseph was able to provide. I felt safe with him because he didn't hit me, yell at me or emotionally abuse me. But I was forever waiting for him to come home at night when he was out binge drinking. One time I even got up in the middle of the night and stood by some neighbour's door in the hallway, trying to hear Joseph's voice. I was a jealous lunatic when it came to my boyfriends, and I'd go to extreme lengths trying to control and monitor their behaviour so I didn't get hurt. I also was struggling with the after-effects of a severe concussion; I would get dizzy if I stood up too fast, forget my words, and anxiety was becoming part of my everyday life.

Joseph and I found a place owned by a sympathetic landlord who agreed to rent the place to us for $620 inclusive. We were ecstatic because it was a really nice place with light pink plush rugs. We didn't have much to our names, just a few ragged pieces of furniture, a floor model TV and a table that I had painted high-gloss black. Over the course of many parties, though, various people had etched their names into the paint. During one particular party, Floyd had used a knife and etched across the whole table "Joseph loves Colleen." It was the tackiest table you've ever seen.

We were happy most of the time. Joseph helped me with

the kids and we anxiously awaited the arrival of the baby in December. Sometimes we would take the kids to the park or just walk around looking in pawnshops to pass time. Joseph doted on the kids and he did not have a mean bone in him but his main fault was being an alcoholic. I could never rely on him to come home or drink just one beer. He would binge for days and come home begging for forgiveness, swearing he would never do it again. I was afraid to be alone and I really loved Joseph very much. He had beautiful long black hair that hung to his waist; this was his best feature. One thing I never noticed about Joseph when we first started going out was that he only had one eye. When he was eighteen years old he'd gone to a party and been stabbed in the eye with a broken beer bottle by someone who was out to get him. I didn't see that missing eye, I just saw a handsome, loving man who would never leave me.

One of the other issues that hung over our relationship was finding out that there was the Canada-wide warrant out on Joseph and he could get picked up at any time. I didn't take it seriously, but we could never get a phone in his name and my name was dirt with the telephone company. I was learning that being a rat had serious consequences and you don't rat out friends, loved ones or gangster-type people. At this point I knew I would never turn Joseph in because I felt I couldn't live without him.

During this year I lived solely on welfare benefits and would take a cab home from grocery shopping at Superstore with a car full of groceries, but it still wasn't enough to get by. I tried to shop well but I didn't know enough about buying groceries, and my cooking skills were limited to Hamburger Helper and other fast-food dishes. We would resort to the food banks when we ran out of food and my aunty would buy us fifty-pound bags of red potatoes from the Hutterites. I ran out of food a lot back in those days — we lived on rice, tomato soup, Kraft Dinner and noodles from the food bank.

December came and I was as big as a house, pregnant with Charmaine. She finally arrived December 12, 1993, after days of labour. By the time it came to push her out I was exhausted. I could barely keep my eyes open but the pain that wracked my body with each contraction whipped me back to reality. She had to have an intervention and the doctor resorted to suction to pull her out. Her poor little head was long and misshapen from being in the birth canal for so long. I was so tired and upset that I couldn't hold her immediately. I just wanted to sleep but the nurses encouraged me to hold her so that we could bond better. It was love at first sight for me and her father! She had a little hat to cover her long head and she began crying, which meant to me that she was healthy. We had a baby for Christmas and she was born exactly one year to the day after her father and I had met.

We settled into the lifestyle of a somewhat functional family. Joseph was good at being a father; he had no problem changing diapers, staying up late with feedings and helping with the other kids. For those few months it was a nice life with very little to complain about. My dad visited me often for coffee and I got to know him a little better; my mom, Esther, was still living on skid row, drinking. She came to stay with me one week, to try to sober up, but she only lasted three days and I could see her getting restless. My mom was quiet when she was sober. She didn't have much to say and I led most of the conversation. I asked her questions about us girls but she couldn't answer them. I just wanted to get to know her better but I think my mom was damaged beyond help. In the grips of addiction she was lost to me. I hated her for what she was because I didn't understand why she just couldn't stop drinking. I had no insight or knowledge of addiction, residential schools or what my mom had been through.

It was about this time that one of Charles's relatives, Janet, contacted me to let me know Charles was getting out of jail and wanting to contact me to see his son, Cree. Part of me was terrified and another part of me couldn't wait to see him again, to see if he had changed. I was praying and hoping he had changed into a good man and that somehow all that time in jail had made him see how violent a person he was. The day finally came when I took a bus across town from the north side of Edmonton to the south, to Janet's house in Millwoods where Charles had been released on probation. I was so nervous to see him, and he was once again buff from working out in jail. I ended up leaving Cree with Charles for the night and going back home to Joseph with my head swimming with lust and desire for Charles. Joseph was pissed that I left Cree for an overnight visit with Charles. I loved Joseph and was happy with him but part of me wanted Charles back. I never cheated on any of my boyfriends, but that night before I left Charles, he had begged me to stay and spend the night with him. I wanted to but my loyalty was with Joseph. I could never cheat on him.

Spring 1994 rolled around and I decided I wanted to go back to work or school. I was tired of sitting around on welfare, always scrounging for money from friends or pawning our TV, stereo or VCR. I went to a local business school called CDI (Career Development Institute) and was approved for a student loan to take Computerized Office Administration. I was back in school once again.

The computer was a new concept for me. The last computer I had been on was an old Apple from school. I was introduced to ACCPAC, Lotus 123 and Accounting. I was doing well and with the student loan our income had increased a little bit. I was able to buy some professional clothes, get the kids into a decent daycare, and go out for lunch occasionally. Joseph got back into drinking occasionally and even I went to the bar on a girls' night out.

But one day we met our neighbours and invited them over for a few beers. The downstairs neighbour, Faye, was babysitting the kids. I don't remember what started the fight between us or maybe I overreacted, but it got pretty heated and it was the first and only time I became afraid of Joseph because he pulled out a knife from the silverware drawer and chased me out of the apartment. I ran down to Faye's apartment and locked the door. Somebody called the police and they came and searched my apartment, but Joseph had fled the scene. I didn't put two and two together but I had unknowingly given up Joseph's location when the police questioned me about who had a knife; I gave them Joseph's name without thinking. The next morning he came home sober and apologetic. I was having a few friends over for coffee and Joseph was reading the paper. Around 11 a.m. I heard a commotion outside and when I looked out the window I saw men dressed in tactical gear, with a SWAT team truck and police dogs. I turned around to tell Joseph but he was already off the couch and gone. Within a minute the police were at my door with their dogs, forcing their way in. They searched my apartment — the oven, the cupboards, under the sink, the bathroom and even in our laundry — for Joseph. I told them he was gone and that I didn't know where he went. Most of the time I did not know where Joseph went anyways so I figured he had gotten away. I later found out he was hiding upstairs with our neighbour Stephanie and her boyfriend. He should have stayed put but he got antsy and ran from there, thinking that they might search everywhere with dogs. He got caught outside and taken down with pepper spray and a dog. I was devastated and knew that I probably would never see him again.

I was able to talk with him when he called from the Remand Centre where he was being held, but he was being shipped back to Regina to face the arson charges. I found out from the detectives who later questioned me that Joseph had been paid to commit arson and burn down a bar/restaurant so the owner could collect the insurance money. He had been paid some of the money for the arson and I remember him buying baby things the previous summer, before I had Charmaine. He bought her a chair to sit in, some clothes and really not that much when I look back. The rest he drank because he went on a binge for weeks.

I didn't realize that money was crime money but the detectives questioned me as to how much I knew about the arson and issued a summons for me to appear as a witness. I discarded the summons, put it away in a drawer somewhere. I never thought of it again until I was arrested for it years later on a bench warrant.

My life quickly unravelled during 1994. I became an alcoholic. I had met most of the people who lived in my building and almost everyone partied. Roxie was down the hall from me and we became close friends. Her boyfriend Gerald used to beat the crap out of her in the hallway, but she was a fighter and most of the time she hit him back. One night she was knocking on my door and had a bottle of wine — she needed a place to chill while Gerald cooled his heels. Roxie would become a lifelong friend and drinking buddy that summer. Man, that girl could fight. She would take on anyone who ever tried to bully me or confront me. She was like a little tornado when she fought, only 5'5" and slim but tough. She was a brawler in the bar and girls didn't mess with her. There weren't many men who would either. I never had to worry when Roxie was around because she always had my back and I always had hers. I was a lookout many times for her — just the size of me back then was enough to keep people from messing with us in the bar.

After Joseph went to jail, I was depressed and drinking away my sorrows with the neighbours. I began to hit the bar more and more each week. Down the street in the neighbour-hood that I lived was a bar called The Cromdale Hotel. It was a seedy, dark, smoky place that played live country music on the weekends. During the week it was dead but Friday night it was a happening place. Lots of Indigenous people went to this bar and I started to meet a lot of people, especially men.

I still attended school but every day after classes I'd walk to the bar and get wasted until I ran out of money or couldn't stand up. I loved the attention I got from men, and when I'd walk into the bar each night I'd be scanning for new and good-looking prospects. After a few drinks all the men were good-looking and I'm sure that worked in their favour also. I started missing a lot of school, hanging out with another classmate, B.J., short for Betty-Jo. She was a rambunctious girl and crazy when she was drunk. She was flirtatious, in your face and wild. One afternoon after school we got wasted in a small bar and lost track of time. B.J. was so drunk she couldn't walk let alone drive so she called her boyfriend Mario to come get her and I walked home drunk. As I passed a yard I heard a bunch of people yell out, "Fuckin' drunken Indians!" I stopped to see who they were yelling at and they said to me, "Get the fuck outta here, wagon burner." I sobered up quickly and walked home as fast as I could.

That incident scared the shit out of me, that someone thought I was a wagon burner and talked to me in such a hate-ful way. Had I become one of those "drunken Indians" like on skid row? Did I look that bad? Why did they hate Indigenous people so much? My self-esteem plunged and I felt a knot in my stomach. That was the first time I experienced racism so bluntly and violently directed at me, and it scared me that maybe next time I would get beat up.

My drinking descended to the point of me staying up all night partying and then trying to go to class. On one particu-lar morning, I had partied with my neighbour Roxie and some other people. I was drinking beer and putting on my makeup, getting ready for school without having a wink of sleep. I stumbled off to school and tried to appear normal. B.J. appealed to me to come have a cigarette with her. She told me I reeked of booze and everyone could smell me but I laughed it off. B.J. also told me she had concert tickets to see Pink Floyd and wanted me to come see it with her. I agreed that I would come but she told me I needed to sleep it off first. After my cigarette I went back up to the classroom but was called into the dean's office. I had a hard time getting there because I fell into the tree in the lobby. The dean was concerned and asked if I was experiencing problems at home. I said yes and made up a lame excuse about problems with the building and my neighbours. I promised that things would get back on track soon. I never went back to school and dropped out of the program.

Things went from bad to worse. I faced an eviction for non-payment of rent. I was partying every day, had lots of people at my place all the time and was relying on Faye to babysit. I was giving her $250 a month to babysit at my beck and call. She basically raised Charmaine during this time. I had hardly any contact with my kids from May to October. I mean, I cooked, cleaned and did the grocery shopping but as soon as those kids were in bed, I'd hit the bar. Faye would stay up all night worrying about me and when I came home the next day I'd be hung over and she would be mad as hell at me. She never confronted me about being a bad parent or a neglectful mother, she just accepted the cash and watched the kids.

I think I had between twenty-five and thirty partners during that summer, and I had no shame because I had no respect or regard for my health, my safety or my worth as a woman. I let these men use my body so I could feel loved, even if it was for five minutes. I was desperate to feel loved but it never came. I even convinced myself that the promiscuity was my way of getting what I wanted from them; I was heartless and conniving in getting whom I wanted and what I wanted. Roxie and I were also scammers and would go to the bar to "mark men in." If we saw a table with men buying lots of booze, we would mark them in by sitting with them, getting them to buy drinks with the offer of maybe something more if they came back to our place. We always got them to buy beer and cigarettes. We always found an excuse to kick that person out of the party, or if they passed out first we shaved their eyebrow or something. One time we even shaved a guy's stomach and drew a happy face on it. Man, I took some serious chances with these men who were strangers to us. They could have seriously hurt us.

One evening Roxie and I had only enough change for one glass of draft. The waitress, being the funny bitch that she was, brought over two straws for us to share the one glass of draft beer. Some men offered to buy us a jug of draft, which tasted nasty, like a dirty ashtray, but we wanted to get drunk. We all drank up and they wanted to go to another bar farther away so we all jumped in their car and took off. They took us to The Crest, which is a seedy bar known for lots of fights but good music. Roxie and I didn't have our IDs on us so we couldn't get in. Those dudes left us at the door and walked away. We were stranded and had about thirty blocks to get back to the Cromdale. We hitchhiked along 118th Avenue, which is fairly busy. A dude in a white Cadillac picked us up and as we were drinking he offered to take us to a party with some other dudes. Then I heard the doors lock — CLICK. I got a bad vibe from this dude and felt like he was up to no good. Roxie was sitting in the front passenger seat and I was right behind her in the back. I reached up and unlocked her door and then mine and at the next red light we bolted from the car at the same time. She must have felt the same way I did. We had heard stories of Indigenous women and women we knew who had been killed and left in fields all around Edmonton. To this day over forty Indigenous women have been murdered by a serial killer (or killers) in the Edmonton area.

I took many chances with many men. Herbie was a guy I met in a bar. He was immediately smitten with me and we danced the night away; he bought all the drinks. We took off to a party with Roxie but ended up getting separated when I went into Herbie's car. I can't remember what happened that night but when I woke up, I was lying in the backseat of Herbie's car, naked, and so was he. A person walking his dog was peeking into the car asking if I was all right. I was embarrassed and disoriented. I can't recall what happened or if I had sex with Herbie, but I assumed we did and he drove me home right after that. He was an extremely handsome Indigenous man, tall, wearing cowboy boots, tight jeans and a gorgeous smile. The next time I saw him he showed up unexpectedly at Roxie's party. Oh man, I was surprised and he smelled so good; he was wearing Eternity perfume for men. We got very drunk that night and ended up sleeping on the floor. Roxie's boyfriend Ernie told me that he caught Herbie taking advantage of me by trying to have sex with me while I was passed out. I didn't believe Ernie, or maybe I didn't want to believe that this man would do that to me. I never saw Herbie again and maybe Ernie was right. We always referred to Herbie as "Hobo Herbie" after that.

Roxie and I would go on adventures downtown, on skid row —a derogatory term we used back in the day for the downtown area of Edmonton where there were seedy bars, lots of poverty, homelessness. We would dress up real nice and go sit in the skid row bars where the crazy, pilled-out drunks were. Roxie knew everybody on the street because her family lived there also. She was hooked up in a way so that no one could touch her because her uncles were known as fighters and her mom was the toughest and meanest on skid row. Roxie's mom had a mullet and she wasn't fat but she was thick. She walked and talked like a man. I remember one hot summer night we were walking around trying to find something to do and there was a soup kitchen truck. Roxie and I sat and had barley soup and a bread roll on the street corner with some street folks — just talking and being real. It was humbling for us to get to know some people who were really hurting. We ended up not drinking that night and just going home. But I saw no way out of this life and accepted it as *my* life. I had no role models to look up to and no hopes or dreams to do better at this point.

During this time I ended up being pregnant with my fourth child and terrified. I sobered up because I had no choice. I was scared this time because I had no partner to help me through the pregnancy. Those were the toughest times I have ever been through. I was alone with three small kids, pregnant, on welfare and terribly poor. I would make forts for my kids, read stories to them and make cookies to pass the time. We never had cable or movies or anything fun to do except what I created. I thought this was how my life was meant to be: a broke-ass Indian living on welfare, just like the stereotype. I didn't want better for myself. I figured I deserved my life for the choices I had made.

I was twenty-two years old and my friends back in Sault Ste. Marie were going to college and university while I took the path of least resistance. I made friends easily wherever I went, but the friends I made were almost always criminals with questionable motives. They always had a hook like scamming, stealing, selling drugs or using. I didn't care as long as they didn't fuck me over. I was a loyal friend and reaped the benefits of having friends in low places. When you have friends in low places nothing is impossible, there are no limits and morality takes a back seat. Survival and instinct trump doing the right thing. I met a girl named Shirley in my building who was a complete freak when she got drunk. She would beat the shit out of her boyfriend and trash her apartment. This would happen every few weeks. One day I had to head downtown for court and she tagged along. We stopped in to use the bathroom in the courthouse and Shirley came across a wallet in her stall. She told me to walk real fast and keep up with her. I had no idea she had found the wallet. We walked a few blocks to a restaurant and went into the bathroom where she searched the wallet and found $360, which we split. Well, karma sucks. I didn't get caught but the universe paid me back. I suffered for two months afterwards, going to food banks and struggling with more poverty for stealing that money.

I decided to move to another apartment down the street. It was a nicer building and my friend Roxie was living there with her partner, Ernie. I was about six months pregnant, with three little ones at home. I had begun proceedings to give the baby up for adoption and had found a family. But I was also having problems with Wayne. He had been taking Naomi on weekends and during that time he set her up real nice in his house. Someone was coaching him on how to get custody of Naomi, but he wasn't smart enough to know that because we didn't have papers drawn up, he had equal access to her. I wasn't much smarter myself; I didn't know I needed paperwork to prove that I was the primary caregiver.

Wayne took her one weekend and never brought her back, and the police would not help me because I needed paperwork to prove I was the primary caregiver. I was distraught that my daughter had been taken from me. I cried for days on end and didn't know what to do. No one would help me or give me answers. The court system seemed like a giant machine of rules with paperwork that needed money to make the machine work. I had no money and Legal Aid was my only option. Those Legal Aid lawyers do their very least to help you. Wayne was granted interim custody of Naomi with weekend visits for me.

I was astonished. How could they take a child away from her mother after four years? But in the court's eyes it was my word against Wayne's and now I had to prove he was a bad parent and didn't deserve to take care of Naomi primarily. This messed my kid up for the next thirteen years, and he did nothing but instill hatred, dysfunction and chaos in her life.

By this time, I was almost thirty-two weeks pregnant, and the stress must have triggered labour because one morning I was in so much pain. My neighbours rushed me to the hospital and later that evening I gave birth to a premature baby girl I named Tara Lynne. They told me she was 22 inches long at thirty-two weeks, which is very long for a baby never mind a premature baby. Most babies are born twenty-one inches at term. That baby girl was perfect when she came out, and she looked like a full-term baby. A neighbour was watching the kids while I was in the hospital. I was torn because I knew I had no help at home and I could barely get by as it was with the three little ones I already had. I had to give Tara Lynne up and hoped she would have a better chance with two parents. The best I could do was hope she was raised right, without abuse or poverty. During my pregnancy I felt like I was making the right decision about giving the baby up, but I was torn because I knew one day she would seek me out and ask the same questions I asked my parents: "Where were you? Why didn't you try to get me back or look for me? Why did you give me up?" Grief and guilt wracked my body as I wondered how I would deal with it if she grew up and hated me. What if she wanted nothing to do with me?

A month after Tara Lynne was born Charles came back into my life. He just showed up one day and wanted to see Cree. I hadn't had much contact with him because I heard he was living with his cousin Dawn and raising her kids. I had trepidations about getting back with Charles but I didn't listen to my gut; I let him back into my life because I was lonely, and his special gift to me was crabs from his past partner. He had crabs so bad they were crawling in his leg hairs. The only way I had noticed was by seeing what looked like a scab on my skin and it turned out to be a crab. They really do look like little crabs. I was disgusted and humiliated because we both had to get prescription medicated shampoo to get rid of it.

Within weeks I was pregnant with my fifth child, Jonathan. Times were different with Charles; he was calmer and had quit drinking but he was still a mean asshole and when he was angry with me he would ignore me for days. I used to see him sit with a cigarette and his coffee, literally ignoring the kids and me until he was ready to talk to me. I constantly worried that Charles would fall off the wagon and come home drunk. If he went to work and was late getting home, I'd be pacing, wondering if I should get out and go to a shelter.

With Charles working temporary landscaping jobs, we were doing better but he only went to work when he felt like it. He got fired not too long after. This man couldn't keep a job if his life depended on it and he blamed the employers for his shortcomings.

I found out from his sister Linda that one time he had a job handing out flyers in neighbourhoods to houses that needed roof repairs. I believed that he was out there earning money but instead he was passed out on his sister's couch and then would come home after five, lying to me and going on about how many flyers he put out. He never got paid for this job because he didn't work and blamed the employer for being shady.

~~~

My surviving sister Dakota would drift in and out of my life at various times, mostly when she needed a place to eat or sleep. There were many times she would show up high at my house. On one occasion she showed up at my basement suite knocking loudly, and when I opened the door, she was high on something and dressed in a pair of knee-high men's socks, no pants or underwear, and a long t-shirt. Dakota had white powder around her mouth like icing sugar and was talking crazy about the police beating her up and dropping her off in a snowbank. She said they took her pants because they were covered in blood from a fight she had witnessed. It didn't make sense and I wanted to call the police but she begged me not to. I didn't have a phone, in any case. I feared the police had hurt my sister after that event and had dropped her off in the snowbank like she had said. I let her sleep it off but it nagged my brain for years that I never said anything.

The next time Dakota came to my place she used my bathroom and fell asleep in the bathtub, naked, with her rigs for shooting up on the bathroom counter. My kids were peeking into the crack where the door was left open and giggling. I slapped my sister's thigh and told her to get up and quit leaving her drugs lying around. Charles didn't like Dakota because she would tell him off, call him names or call him on being an abusive boyfriend. I was such an idiot that I begged her not to get him mad because I knew Charles would take it out on me later. Finally, it got to the point where he told me Dakota was no longer welcome in our house.

Not too long after this Dakota was assaulted badly by a john or pimp or someone she either stole drugs off or owed money to. They hurt her bad. The hospital called to tell me she needed a safe place to stay but I couldn't help because Charles didn't want her there, so I had to say no. Letting my sister down twisted my stomach into knots of guilt and it was a feeling that stayed with me because I always felt responsible for the bad things that happened to my sisters, like I should have done more.

~ ~ ~

It's such a cruel irony that in the same year I gave up a baby for adoption, I became pregnant with another child. Jonathan was born in May 1996 and I was ecstatic to have another boy. He was a very long baby with big hands and feet and long arms and legs. He was the spitting image of his father and *mooshum*. At four months old the doctor told us he was in the ninety-sixth percentile for his height and head circumference and would tower over kids his age.

Charles was a doting father at times, very proud of his sons but also hard on Cree at the tender age of three. Charles would mock him if he cried, telling him that men don't cry and macho things that strike fear in the hearts of mothers. A mother's instinct is to soothe, coddle and never let her child experience hurt. I knew Cree loved his dad so much and wanted to make sure he never disappointed him, even at the age of three.

Things at home were relatively good considering I lived with someone who had almost killed me in previous years. There was no physical abuse but lots of worrying and anxiety when Charles didn't come home, for fear he *would* come home and kill me this time in a drunken rage. He was still sober, with only one incident where he didn't come home. On that occasion he was supposed to go pay the rent and come home but he never came back and by ten at night I was worried he would arrive back drunk and kill me. I packed up the kids and caught a cab to the closest shelter. I found out later that Charles had been picked up by the police for a fine he still owed. I was hasty in my decision to go to a shelter and I remember telling the shelter workers that he only beat me when he was drunk. They wanted to do a safety plan with me before I left but I told them I hid knives around the house under towels, in my sock drawer and under my side of the bed, and that was my safety plan.

Time flew by and that summer we both enrolled into college

courses to start in the fall of 1996. At first going to school was fun but soon I began to experience severe panic attacks and anxiety on the LRT train, which is like a subway. I began to dread going to school. Once I got to class and was seated, I started panicking there too, overcome with anxiety. My mouth would start to water, dizziness and nausea took over and I'd fight to normalize my breathing, but that would become a fight also! Fight or flight instinct took over and flight would always win. It got to the point that I couldn't even go grocery shopping without Charles. I would leave my cart with the groceries still in it and flee the store when I felt a panic attack coming on. My hands would get sweaty, I would start feeling jittery and dizzy, and I was afraid I'd vomit or pass out so I would run out of the store. Once I got out of the situation I immediately felt better. Crowds, trains, buses, stores and the mall became unbearable. I was starting to become an agoraphobic and crippled by anxiety. I could no longer attend classes because I couldn't catch the train downtown and it was too far to walk. Medication was prescribed to me for anxiety and depression, but this medication made me feel foggy, slow and disoriented. All I did was sleep and in one month I lost twenty-five pounds. The irony of this crippling anxiety is that during this time I was due to get married to Charles.

He had proposed to me in class in front of our classmates and I accepted even though I felt he was showing off for attention. Our wedding was set for November 30, 1996. We had a small ceremony in our townhouse with friends and family. I bought a huge cake, ordered trays of meats and cheeses, and bought matching dark green dresses for the girls and white shirts and black dress pants for the boys. By this time, marrying Charles felt like an obligation. If I said no, I was sure he would kill me —I don't think rejection would have sat well with him. The violence I had experienced from him stayed with me even though he had not recently threatened to kill me. My anxiety was at its maximum height during this time — I was experiencing weird delusions and believed I was being haunted by an entity. It was the medication that was fucking my head up.

November 1996 to February 1997 was a pilled-up delusional mess. On one occasion I ended up in downtown Edmonton in a neighbourhood called Little Italy but had no clue as to how I got there. I remember asking a bus driver how to get home but was afraid to get on the bus. I called my house from a payphone and Charles took a bus to come get me. We walked twenty-five blocks home because I was insistent not to get back on a bus for fear of a panic attack. Blackouts were becoming common on this medication; I decided to stop taking the pills because they were making things worse.

Charles and I moved to a different apartment building that year because as usual we couldn't pay rent or got behind on rent. Eventually I got a job working as a dishwasher in a local restaurant a block away. My boss was all right at first; he began to train me as a waitress and then as a cook; my multi-tasking skills were phenomenal and I danced circles around the cook and him when it came to managing dishwashing and waitressing, then cooking. I was doing all right making money, gaining skills, and my anxiety wasn't as bad because I could walk to work. My kids were in daycare and Charles was training to be a wildfire fighter. It seemed like all the Native guys in Edmonton were wildfire fighters; they would train for a few weeks then go to the camps up North for two or three weeks.

During this time, I became pregnant again: Charles didn't believe in birth control so I wasn't allowed to take it. While he was gone up North to work in the wildfire camps, I miscarried. I had three small children in my care and the stress must have been too much. My job consisted of me standing and walking for eight hours a day, dropping my kids off in the morning and picking them up after work. On this particular day I was getting a bowl of ice cream ready for a customer. I leaned over the deep freeze to get the ice cream and felt something come out of my vagina. This feeling was alien to me but if I had to describe it, I think it was the beginning of a fetus. I ran to the staff bathroom and felt something drop into the toilet bowl, but it slipped down before I could catch a glimpse. The cramps started and I began to bleed heavily, and for about fifteen minutes I stayed bent over from the contractions. My boss was knocking on the door, asking if was okay and if I needed an ambulance. Embarrassed and modest, I asked him to get the cook, who was a woman. She gave me two aprons to cover the front and back of me so I could walk home. It was only ten minutes, but the cramping forced me to stop and breathe through it like labour, each cramp forcing more blood out.

By the time I made it to my apartment building, I was bleeding profusely. I called my babysitter Faye who rushed over and by the time she got there I was in serious trouble — the chair I was sitting in was soaked with blood and I was losing consciousness. Faye was screaming "Oh my god, Colleen, oh my god!" in terror from seeing so much blood on the floor and chair. I called 911, told them I was bleeding badly and felt the walls of unconsciousness closing in, making everything grey. It felt like a tunnel with the voices beside me sounding far away. Within minutes I could hear a siren and I was in and out of consciousness. Then all of a sudden I was being stood up to walk to a stretcher and I literally bled a bucket of blood. It is the most unnatural sensation to feel massive blood loss out of your own body and have no control over it. Each contraction pushed more and more blood out — I was hemorrhaging to death. In the ambulance my lips and body couldn't stop shivering from being in shock and I asked the attendant if I was going to die. He replied, "We are going to do our best to make sure you don't."

This was not the answer I was hoping for, I wanted a solid "No, you're not going to die Colleen." I told him he looked like the head vampire guy from the vampire movie called *The Lost Boys*, and he laughed loudly. Then he told me a joke to make me laugh. He asked me, "What is the difference between a guy with a tie and a horse's tail?" I said, "What?" He replied, "The horse's tail covers the whole asshole." This time I laughed loudly. He knew I had gone into shock and he was trying to keep me calm and distracted. It worked.

At the hospital, they rushed me into surgery, and when I woke up later the first thing I heard was my husband Charles yelling at the nurses, demanding to know where I was. I had told the paramedics that my husband was a firefighter up North, so they contacted him somehow and flew him in by helicopter. Do you know that fucker blamed me for losing his job? He didn't care that I almost died, he was upset that he had to leave his job to come see me. I later learned from someone else who worked with him that he didn't lose his job, he just didn't want to go back once my crisis was over. I was his scapegoat to quit.

My doctor told me my baby-making days were over and I told him that my husband wouldn't let me get my tubes cut or take birth control. He advised me to be careful, but Charles refused to wear condoms so I tried my best to not let him ejaculate inside of me, feigning periods and headaches to get out of having sex with him. The trauma of having excruciating cramps and bleeding uncontrollably left me feeling cautious about becoming pregnant again.

The restaurant I worked at began to draw an Indigenous crowd because I worked there. It drew the attention of a famous Indigenous country band called C-Weed, and the leader, Errol Ranville, would come in every morning with his band and eat breakfast. My boss, Clem, would call them a bunch of travelling gypsies but in all reality Errol Ranville was a successful businessman. They were trying to set up a music club venue that featured Indigenous bands from all over. I got to know them and one day they asked if I got to keep my tips. I said no, Clem makes me give them to the cook. Errol said I should be able to keep the tips and then he offered me a job to work as a kitchen manager in his new bar, and any tips I made I could keep.

Charles was not happy about this at all. He didn't want me working in a bar but I assured him everything would be all right. It was good money and I was ecstatic to be a kitchen manager. Errol warned me not to get caught up partying with the rest of the staff. "Just do your job and you'll do well," he said. At first things were good at C-Weed's; making hamburgers, hot dogs, French fries, poutine and fast food was easy money. I was making $100 to $200 a night in profit and tips. Things changed in my life when some idiot pulled the fire alarm at closing time and the fire trucks came. All the staff stayed and waited for the alarm to get shut off before we locked up. The bouncers drove my co-worker and me home and I guess Charles had stayed up waiting for me and saw me getting out of a truck. I was yanked into the house and thrown across the room onto the couch. Charles got up in my face and went through my purse, throwing my lipstick and lighter at me. He forced me into the bathroom and stood me in front of the mirror and made me cut off my hair. I was left with hair so short I looked like a man. Charles told me no one would want me and I believed him.

The next morning he took the kids to daycare while I slept. I had no idea what was to come next. My husband came into our bedroom and from the end of the bed tore the covers off of me and pulled my pajama bottoms off while I struggled to keep them on. I was groggy from sleep and disoriented. While he was doing this he was talking about how I never give him sex anymore, and who the hell was I fucking? This was not done in an act of passion or foreplay; he was angry and hell-bent on getting it in. He forced me over onto my stomach and I was terrified by now. Charles was being rough with me and he forced himself on me and entered my anus and tore me. I was crying and begging him to stop because it hurt. I was afraid of him and of making him angrier and knew his beatings could be brutally violent. After a few minutes he was done and I scurried into the bathroom, shaking and hurt. My ass was bleeding and felt ripped open. I wasn't sure what had just happened. How could a husband do that to his wife? Is he allowed to hurt me like that? Was that rape? Would someone believe me that my husband had raped me? I yelled at him from the bathroom, "You hurt me, I'm bleeding," but he didn't respond. Charles stewed for the rest of the day and when it was time to pick up the kids, he told me I was going with him. Charles wasn't employed and would sit around all day so it was his responsibility to pick up the kids after daycare. I wasn't allowed to go to work that evening at C-Weed's and Charles told me I wasn't going anywhere, he wanted me to quit my job at the bar.

At this point, I was taking care of my own children as well as my late sister Gina's kids, whose father had abandoned them. I later arranged for them to live with one of their aunts on their dad's side, but at this point, we were all trapped. I could have tried to run but I was afraid of what might happen. I think Charles knew he had fucked up and that if I left, I would go to the police. The next day, after the kids went to daycare, Charles attacked me in the kids' bedroom and raped me on my daughter's bed. He was very sick about it this time and was smelling my underwear and checking it for "cum stains." He held me down on the bed and forced himself onto me again. I lay there and took it like a dead fish, tuning myself out. Why didn't I run? What the heck was I doing? Charles ejaculated and pushed me away like he was disgusted with me. I was screaming inside my head "Run, get out!" but I knew he wouldn't let me leave.

Later that afternoon we brought the kids home and Charles's brother Jermaine stopped by. I knew Jermaine wouldn't let anything happen to us. I took all the kids and ran up the street to my friend Faye's apartment. Charles chased us but gave up because I think it drew attention to him. I ran those kids so fast, pulling their little arms, and they had no idea why they were running from their dad. Faye let us stay but Charles rang the apartment buzzer all night long and in the morning Faye wanted us to leave because she was afraid her landlady would complain. I was mad at her for making us leave, so I crept over to another friend Angela's apartment a block over. She had a one-bedroom apartment with three kids. Charles found me there and called the police, claiming I stole his children.

I was in a jam; I didn't want him to get in trouble, I just wanted to get away from him. When the police came to question me at Angela's house they asked me what was going on. I brought one of the officers who was female to the bedroom and told her how Charles had hurt me and that I didn't know if that was rape or not. The officer said it definitely was and that I needed to be examined because my anus had been ripped. My children and I were taken to a women's shelter and a nurse examined me. I had to fill out paperwork and then the police informed me they had a four-year-old bench warrant for me. I was arrested the next day at the shelter in front of my kids and taken to the justice of the peace.

I had never been to jail, worn handcuffs or travelled in a cruiser before. I was brought to the police station and processed in the basement; I had to lift my breasts and surrender my bra and shoelaces; I was amused. After this intrusive act, I was put into a holding cell. It was boring and claustrophobic, the cell walls were covered with the names of past prisoners and I found Charles's name etched into the paint. The shittiest part about this whole ordeal was being arrested in front of my kids, who didn't understand what was happening. The shelter staff took care of them while I dealt with the warrant. That warrant was issued back in 1994, when Joseph was picked up by the SWAT team, and he had already served his time by then. The judge threw it out and considered it a waste of time that I was arrested and brought in.

Finally, after a few tense days waiting in the shelter, we got word from the police that I could go home. Charles was picked up after a standoff outside the house, police surrounded the place we lived in and he finally agreed to come out. He was charged with one count of sodomy and sexual assault against me, and child welfare was brought in to consult with me because he raped me in my kid's bed.

I fell off the wagon again for a while — my dad shook his head at me but I didn't care. Drinking was my escape and when I returned to work at the bar it was only a matter of weeks before I lost my job and became a customer at C-Weed's Cabaret.

Charles was locked up and I was partying and drinking every day, and one day a police officer showed up to talk to me. Her name was Constable Wolf and she had stopped by to see how I'd been doing since the assault. I told her about drinking and working at the bar, getting fired and having no direction. She told me, "Colleen you're too damn smart to be working in a bar and you deserve better." She also gave me a warning and an eye opener. Officer Wolf told me that if I took Charles back when he got out of jail, child protection workers would apprehend my kids because he was a danger to them and me. That sobered me straight up and I thought to myself, "Fuck that! No one is taking my kids from me!"

# CHAPTER 7

# E-tipayimsoowin

SOBERING UP WAS NOT easy. All my friends drank and went to the bar every weekend. I couldn't visit any friends who didn't have beer or whiskey in their house. Sometimes anger would boil up inside of me because I felt like I was missing out on something, but nobody missed me anyways. I found a job working part-time in a second-hand bookstore called the Wee Book Inn, which specialized in buying, selling and trading used books, comics, magazines and CDs. This is when my love affair with books really took off. I had always loved reading but being surrounded by books was a dream come true, and I spent my time organizing and re-shelving second-hand books.

It was good for a few weeks but I had a hard time finding a babysitter in the evening and resorted to using a girl I didn't really know, someone my friend Roxie had recommended. The girl showed up and seemed like she was okay to watch the kids; she didn't seem impaired. I left the kids in her care and went to work a short 5 p.m. to 8 p.m. shift. At 6 p.m. my landlady called to tell me that my kids, who were eighteen months, three and four years old, were running up and down the hallway, had cut off all their hair and were not being watched. It took me ten minutes to walk home from work to find my babysitter passed out on the couch. I slapped her across the face to wake her up.

I said, "Look at my fuckin' kids you bitch!" They were standing in the living room with their hair cut off. Cree had cut off all of Charmaine's hair, Charmaine had cut off Jonathan's and Cree's hair, and they all had bald patches on their heads.

Honestly I didn't know whether to laugh or cry. I think I laughed but I was more upset that they had been unsupervised and playing with scissors, running in the hallways. I had to take my kids to a hair salon to get their heads shaved completely and Charmaine looked like a boy. I made a call to my welfare worker, telling her I had to quit my job because I couldn't find good child care. She threatened me and said, "If you quit your job I'll cut off your cheque." I told her, "Listen, what am I supposed to do, leave my kids alone?" and hung up on her. She called child welfare on me and reported me for threatening to leave my kids alone. The next morning I had two child welfare workers knocking at my door. I was fed up and told them my situation and that I'd never leave my kids alone. They asked me what I needed and I told them that honestly, I needed to get out of there and go back to Sault Ste. Marie. After some bureaucratic garbage, welfare agreed to pay my way back to Sault Ste. Marie on the train. At first they wanted to send me on the Greyhound bus, but I was like, "Lady, have you ever ridden for three days on a bus with three kids and no running water? How would you like to go through that?" They relented and paid for a sleeper car on Via Rail for the kids and me.

It was around this time that I learned my sister Gina's kids' temporary stay with their dad's family had broken down and they were back in foster care. I called my adoptive mother Mary to talk about this situation, to see if she could help me make arrangements to bring Jonah and Cheyenne to Sault Ste. Marie also. She told me she had decided to apply for custody of the two kids. My sister would have rolled over in her grave at the thought of our adoptive mother taking custody of her children, but I wasn't in any position at the time to help — I could barely manage my own life and sobriety. I had no choice but to hope for the best.

Leaving was bittersweet. I was happy to get away from Edmonton and all my troubles, but I also had to leave my daughter Naomi behind with her father. I had spent years trying to regain custody of her after Wayne stole her from me, but I was out of options and I knew he would never let me take Naomi with me back to Ontario. Wayne was supposed to bring her to the train station to say goodbye but he never showed up. The last time I had seen Naomi was in 1998, when she was eight years old. At that time I tried to believe that she would be better off with her father; already Wayne had planted the seeds of hate in Naomi by telling her I didn't want her. I wouldn't see her again until 2004. Every day in between I worried about her. I dreamt and prayed for her to come back to me.

~~~

Just before my departure from Edmonton, Gina came to me in a dream. We were walking down Jasper Avenue in downtown Edmonton on a hot sunny day. She was pushing her daughter Cheyenne's stroller and we were talking. I remember her saying to me "Why don't you come see me any more?" Her voice was crystal clear and it woke me up right out of my dream. I hadn't heard my sister's voice in over eight years so to me it was a sign her spirit had visited me.

Before I left, I asked my father to take me to Gina's gravesite. I had never been back since the day she was buried and never really accepted that she was gone. Now I felt like I was abandoning my sister and grief brought me to my knees. I lay my head down on Gina's grave and wept for all the things I would never do with her, and for the children she would never raise. I told her spirit that I would not waste my life, that I'd do better in her name. I promised I would call on her when I needed help and would honour her name and her memory so that no one forgot about her. That day was more painful than the day we buried her because it was then that I truly began to grieve the loss of my sister.

~~~

We had to leave Edmonton within a week. I found out someone was moving into our building from a women's shelter so I invited her over and told her to take everything she needed: beds, linen, dishes, whatever I had she could take. Her teenagers helped themselves and cleaned the apartment out. They were grateful and I was happy to get rid of my stuff.

I needed to skip town without paying rent or bills, so we snuck out that evening. I dragged my duffel bag down the hallway and my cousin Melvin met me in the parking lot. The kids were excited and even though I told them we were going on a train ride, it wasn't real for them until we got to the train station. This was a terrifying day for me, going into the unknown and being responsible for three young human beings.

The train ride must have been amazing for the kids to experience with their young minds and curious eyes. Via Rail had porters who came and folded the bed down to a double berth, and the top bunk pulled out of the ceiling. The kids and I would stare out of the big window up at the stars until the train rocked us to sleep. The dining car was like something out of a movie, with its elegant dishes and place settings; even the butter was put into special dishes and displayed as little balls too precious to eat. Most of the dishes on our table had to be taken away because I didn't want the kids breaking anything. During the train ride it was gruelling trying to keep three children busy, so we would look out the window, counting animals, telephone poles or playing games on the table. I was a smoker and going three days without a cigarette was driving me batty; several times I wanted to sneak into the bathroom for a drag of my smoke but my fear of being thrown off the train was stronger than my need for a smoke. Sleep was an escape from the stress of worrying and boredom.

Heading back to Sault Ste. Marie Ontario was a hasty decision; I had no idea what I was going back to. I wondered how things would be between my adoptive mother and me, as well as with my childhood friends Carla and Nicky. They were now college and university graduates with good jobs. They both had vehicles, stable incomes and were connected to the Sault Ste. Marie community. As my train pulled into Sudbury, Ontario, three days later, my adoptive mother was waiting for us. She looked so much older than when I had last seen her. She had long grey hair, her back was bowed over but she was energetic and happy to see my kids. We had to drive three hours north back to Sault Ste. Marie because the train didn't stop there. The drive was exhausting, and the conversation was mostly catching up and small talk.

Eventually we arrived in the "Soo," the very city I had escaped ten years prior. My childhood friends greeted me at my mom's house, it was strange seeing them as grown adults. I thought they were so sophisticated looking — pangs of inadequacy invaded my thoughts. Carla was tall, well over six feet, gorgeous, with long dark hair, brown skin and big white teeth with a perfect smile. Nicky looked the same but more adult — she reminded me of Rachel from *Friends* with her looks. They had baked a cake to welcome the kids and me and we hugged tightly. The kids and I were exhausted and ready for bed, but my mom gave me a flashlight and said, "You're sleeping in Gramma's old house." I was stunned and disheartened; I wanted to sleep in a nice comfy bed, not a musty old one with squeaky springs. Worse yet, my kids had no beds so we all slept on the floor. I was miserable the first couple of days, sick from the change of weather, and sleeping on the floor didn't help. That first night was very hard; it was so quiet and there was not a stitch of light outside. Gramma's house was old and sat about twenty feet across the property on my mom's lot. It had only cold water in the taps, and for some reason blackflies littered the floor all the time. I was constantly sweeping up dead blackflies and by that evening there would be fifty more.

My mom lived in a rural setting. There were no sirens screaming at all hours of the night, no traffic lights, street lights or airplanes. It was dead quiet except for an occasional bark in the night from dogs in the distance (or maybe wolves? Coyotes?). I was terrified of the silence. All my adult life in Edmonton I had been surrounded in noise, background noise that I was not aware of until it was gone. Pure silence is scary because you don't even know if it's really silence or if you have lost your hearing. I could hear a piercing noise as my ears strained for familiar sounds, even the buzzing of a light post would give me comfort, yet nothing. Silence enveloped me that night and I lay awake waiting for morning, terrified of hearing nothing.

My mom's place was on the edge of the city, not close to a bus stop, so the only way I could get into town was to ask her for a ride or walk down the highway for twenty minutes to the closest city bus stop. I hated living at my mom's. I was completely dependent on her for rides, food and shelter, plus she wanted me to go back to school to become a card dealer for the new casino coming in. I didn't want to work in a casino or deal cards — that sounded like the most boring thing in the world, kind of like math. I was considering joining the army but there was no one to take care of my kids while I went to training camp. Living at my mom's was getting harder and harder, and I was bored, restless and isolated. I had no friends and no money. Both my childhood friends had their own lives and full-time jobs so I didn't see them very much. I needed to live in town but I didn't want to hurt my mom's feelings.

As I said earlier, one afternoon my mom's sister Allison asked me some questions about why my sisters and I left home so young. To hear my Aunty Allison tell me that my mother never told her family that Ronald abused us girls rocked my soul. Anger boiled my blood and I told her the truth of the beatings and sexual abuse. This motivated me to move out of my mom's house. I never confronted her but I sure held a grudge against her for a long, long time.

I found a two-bedroom place in town for my kids and me and bought some bunk beds. My mom gave me a small black and white television that got two channels with the antenna. Once I had my kids enrolled in school I had a bit of freedom during my days to get things done. I went to the courthouse and inquired about the records of my adoptive father's charges. I needed to see them with my own eyes. I took the copy of the records to a lawyer and inquired about suing or charging Ronald for the havoc he created in my sisters' and my life. I wanted him to pay for it. The lawyer told me there is a statute of limitations as to what people can be charged with. The only thing I could do was pursue Criminal Compensation. So I wrote to Criminal Compensation and was sent back massive amounts of paperwork to be filled out — it seemed hopeless at the time. To receive compensation, there needed to be documentation of the crime, counsellor intervention, lists of prescriptions taken, any injuries sustained, etc. This sounded like fresh hell to me. How was I supposed to get this done? I couldn't even talk about the abuse let alone get help for it. I had to find a counsellor, so I called around and found someone who would take me on and navigate the paperwork for compensation. To do this, we had to delve into the abuse I went through with Charles, in addition to that of my adoptive father Ronald White.

One takeaway skill I learned during that time was how to manage the anxiety attacks and develop new techniques by breathing in through my nose and out through my mouth. Wiggling and counting my toes to distract my mind helped also. Practicing the breathing exercises helped me when a panic attack came on suddenly, and eventually taking the bus and going on outings became bearable. But talking about the abusive episodes in my counselling sessions made me breathless, tearful and brought me right back to those terrifying moments. Little did I know at the time I was suffering from Complex Post Traumatic Stress Disorder (C-PTSD), which was diagnosed fifteen years later. I also had not dealt with the loss of my sister Gina and still could not talk about her death so I put that on the shelf and dealt with the abuses from my husband and adoptive father.

Going to see a counsellor was intimidating; you don't know what kind of questions they will be asking or what is expected. I found it awkward at first, like being forced to find something to talk about. For the most part I just tried to talk about superficial matters but eventually the abuse at the hands of my husband and adoptive father started to come out. At that time my insight into the abuse I endured was limited and all I could do was talk about the actual physical acts of violence rather than my emotions of terror and how it impacted my life. The counsellor never really got to hear the parts about when I hid knives around my house to protect myself in case my husband ever got out of jail. Or how sometimes a slight noise would wake me in the middle of the night, causing me to grab a weapon in fear that he had found me, even when I lived thousands of kilometres away from him. Those things never came out because my fear of having my children taken away from me was always in the back of my head, so I was careful about what I said to whom. Performing as a "functional" abused person was exhausting because I had to look at all the angles and consider the risks of exposing my weaknesses.

My sister Dakota followed me back to Sault Ste. Marie from Edmonton. She arrived in December 1998 and went right into a shelter with her daughter Janna and son Chase — my biological father had been raising her son and had given him back to her. The shelter set her up with household furniture, dishes and beds and she moved in right across the hall from me in my apartment building. Why hadn't I thought of getting help from the shelter? Dakota was good at working the system and when she first arrived back in the Soo, we had a good relationship and she managed to stay sober for a few months. But by February she was hitting the bar and bringing home men. One night she brought home a former childhood neighbour of ours, Jack. She brought him over to say hi to me but I didn't have much to say to him. I gave him a coffee and we played some cribbage. He would visit me, bring his DVD player and DVDs over to watch movies all night, and eventually we started dating. At the time he had a job working as a fuel truck driver and owned a car and he was good to me. Jack would drive me to get groceries, help me run errands and visit me daily, and he got along well enough with the kids. He wasn't a drinker or into drugs, which I liked, and for the most part I was happy with him at the time. Everyone else in my building drank and would ask me to babysit on welfare cheque days. I hated it but liked the extra money. I began to make plans to move out. The welfare parties were terrible; kids would be running up and down the hallways and stairs all night while the parents partied away. There were fights, broken bottles and vomit in the laundry room.

During this time, I found out my birth mother had died in the hospital. It was January 1999. I could not go to the funeral in Saddle Lake, Alberta, nor did I want to. I felt nothing at the time. I mean, I was sad that she died but I could not mourn someone

I did not know. I often question myself as to why I didn't cry or grieve the loss of my birth mother at that time.

~~~

In 1999 I was invited to an Adoptee workshop at Sault College and met the Native staff there. One of the women I met was Barb Nolan, a First Nations guidance counsellor who inspired me to go back to school. She sat down with me and together we figured out a path to get me into college. Barb had a welcoming, encouraging manner and a way of making people feel comfortable and safe. She convinced me that I really could succeed. By this time I had been sober for two years and I wanted better for my children and myself.

I enrolled in the Native Community Worker Addictions Counsellor Diploma Program at Sault College in the summer of 2000 and began classes in September.

That summer I also challenged myself to take a class to learn how to ride a motorbike, with Jack's urging. It was very hard to ride a motorbike because the clutch and brake were difficult to master. At one point during the class I was riding a 250cc motorbike and somehow let the clutch out and revved the gas. That bike took off out from under me and I was holding onto the handlebars and running behind it. I was screaming for help and threw the motorbike on the ground, which landed at the feet of my instructor. To top things off, I was the only girl in my class so I had a bunch of men staring at me, laughing, while I was in tears and shaking. I had to sit down to calm my nerves. One of the instructors came over and sat on the pavement with me. He kind of blocked me so the guys couldn't see me crying but it was too late, my pride was hurt. The instructor told me "You got to get back on that bike Colleen. If you don't do it now you will always be scared of it." I dusted myself off, wiped my tears, picked up my bike and completed the rest of the weekend course. But I was always afraid of the bike after that and I never did ride again. I had bought a Honda 250cc before I got my M licence and sold it about six months later.

Classes started and the first day was a confusing mess of trying to find the rooms, get my books and navigate my way through the packed hallways of Sault College. Going back to school in your late 20s amid a lot of younger folks was interesting. I felt very old compared to my younger schoolmates. Thankfully, in my program specifically, we were all Indigenous and in our late twenties, thirties and even forties. My courses in that first year consisted of English Communications, Computers, Psychology, Holistic Health and Addictions. There were approximately forty Indigenous students who started the Addictions Counsellor program together, but after two years at Sault College, only twelve of us graduated. I thought it was going to be easy; the schoolwork wasn't as hard as the emotional work it took to get through the course. There is an old saying, "You can't help anyone until you help yourself," and it was never truer than for this course. If you had demons and unresolved issues of grief, addiction, co-dependency and loss that you had not dealt with, you either sorted it out or quit the program, it was that simple. No one said you had to leave because you had unresolved issues; the students made that decision themselves. The course content was deep, intimate and gruelling, and it forced us to examine our own lives.

We had sharing circles that required us to sit in a circle with our classmates and pass a feather around, everyone taking turns sharing something about ourselves. At first everyone would say "pass" or just stare at the feather, wondering what to say. The thing with a sharing circle was no one else could talk or interrupt you when it was your turn; everyone listened, and what happened in the circle stayed in the circle. It was designed to build trust amongst our group. I dreaded the sharing circle; I had a fear of speaking in front of people. I could feel my stomach turning, my palms sweating and dizziness taking over. I was so worried about what people would think of me or how I looked. I would make superficial comments about being "thankful" or talk about my weekend but eventually it came around to talking about things that I had never spoken about before. I cried, my voice shaking with grief, as I talked about my sisters, my family and my abuse. Classmates bonded, and we learned about each other's most intimate pain and how to sit with each other while we grieved. We learned to just listen and not stop classmates from experiencing their grief or trying to fix it. It was uncomfortable at first to hear people cry and to watch their pain. I had always been afraid of grief. It never got to the point where I was completely comfortable seeing someone in pain but at least I could understand it and not fear it. I still have a hard time watching men cry and grieve; it brings me to tears.

I began to heal but something even more valuable was happening: I was learning spirituality, language and culture. In my whole life I had never been exposed to smudging, praying, sweat lodge, ceremonies or any teachings about our Creator. Can you imagine going your whole life not knowing your *own* culture? I think back to my birth family in Edmonton: none of them knew how to do those things either and could never share them with me. Colonialism through residential schools and Christianity had really done a lot of damage to my family and to many other Indigenous families. Many cultures have been colonized but really, how many had their language forbidden and spiritual practices wiped out on their own homelands? Anger began to brew in my stomach at this realization that our pain and losses were deliberate.

I was afraid the first time I was introduced to smudging with sage. It was new and didn't make sense to me. What did this mean? How did it help me? My senses went into overload from the smell of sage burning and watching the teacher show us the ritual of cleansing our mind, body and soul so that we could see, feel, hear and speak good things. When it was my turn to smudge, fear crept into my heart — what if I looked stupid or I did it wrong? My hands tried to mimic the motions of the smudging ritual that my teacher had done, while my mind raced with wild thoughts: "Am I going to get high? Is this going to work? How can smoke cleanse anything? People are going to know I'm not a real Indian!"

Along with smudging, the Native Education department also had visiting Elders come in to do certain cultural ceremonies. It was always exciting because it meant no classes, but we got a different kind of schooling. It meant sitting, watching, listening and learning for hours, for as long as it took the Elders to smoke their pipes and pray. It was an endurance test and it tried my patience. I couldn't tell if I liked it or not at the time. The Elders would set out their items on blankets in front of them but they gave no explanation as to what the things were or why they did what they did. Part of me admired their items and wanted my own: it would mean I was a true Indian if I had a feather, a pipe and sacred items. We were told not to touch their items, and fear of embarrassment or admonishment in front of my peers kept me from asking questions. Anxiety also kept me from approaching Elders, who I believed had special powers to see right through me and know my thoughts, and I was afraid they would see that I wasn't truly an Indian because I was raised by white people. The shame of not knowing my ceremonies, what the items were and being afraid of Elders kept me from accessing certain ceremonies like sweat lodges or full moon ceremonies for many years. Being apprehensive of my culture sounds bizarre, especially after being kept away from it until then, but part of me did not feel like I belonged. Also I didn't want to appear stupid and they would certainly know that I did not belong if I started asking questions. When you don't know what you don't know, how do you know what to ask?

Along with these new experiences and emotions came understanding about the history of my people and all that they had been through in the treaty-making process, the residential schools and life on the reserves. My education also gave me greater understanding of my mother, father and sisters, and of their pain and suffering. For the longest time I just accepted being a victim of circumstances. I had believed that we deserved the violence, poverty and discrimination we experienced. Everything I learned before college taught me that Indigenous people were inferior, thanks to the state, the media and the Canadian education system as well as my adoptive parents, brother, aunties, uncles and all who contributed to my desperately ignorant upbringing.

The newly found knowledge of the treaties and wealth generated from our negotiated treaties pivoted my life in a new direction, one that straightened my back and gave me the courage to walk proudly with my head held high.

Shortly after starting college, a teacher in one of my classes on Aboriginal history informed us about resource revenue sharing and the Indian Trust, and how every single tree cut, diamond mined, mineral, oil or gas extracted on treaty-negotiated land belonged to First Nations people, and a percentage, now amounting to billions of dollars, is supposed to be shared with bands. The other portion finances the country known as Canada. Canada had been built on the backs of Indigenous dehumanization and suffering and is continually financed through our treaty-making process. Without our resources, Canada would cease to exist. We agreed to share the land and resources in exchange for certain allotments and benefits. We did not agree to live in poverty and struggle on our homelands. I was in shock; my heart skipped a beat with excitement because no one had ever told me this before. I felt like I had some secret information but the larger nagging problem was, why was this not common knowledge? Why did Canadians still believe their taxes pay for First Nations to receive medicines, prescriptions, glasses and education?

I began to share the knowledge I was gaining in college but most people wanted to argue with me. No one wanted to hear the truth and worse yet, no one wanted to hear it from an Indian. It didn't matter to me because I was no longer intimidated by non-Indigenous people trying to cut me down by telling me their taxes paid for my education. I stood up for myself when I felt I was being discriminated against, especially when it came to using my status card for tax exemption. One time I was in Zellers paying for my purchases and I produced my status card, which entitles me not to pay provincial sales tax. A woman behind me in line made an exasperated sound. I turned around and asked her if there was a problem. The lady was embarrassed and said "No," but I was ready to talk about her problem and educate her about my status card.

This knowledge gave me empathy for my own and my family's struggles with addictions but also for how our lives were incredibly disrupted by the Canadian government's attempt to assimilate us. As hard as it is to admit, empathy has never been a strong gift of mine; in fact it ceased to exist until a few years ago. Showing empathy meant being vulnerable and at the time I wasn't ready to be vulnerable to anyone. Showing vulnerability meant weakness and weakness meant feeling emotions and unpredictability. Control was my most valued confidante and I wasn't ready to give that up at the time. But this newly found insight led me to finally understand my mother's life and the loss of her. It helped me deal with my guilt for being so angry with her for her alcohol and substance addictions and for blaming her for us being adopted so far away. It hurt my heart to know that my mother suffered in her childhood and young adult life and that she probably did want to be a good parent who loved her children but was incapable due to atrocities committed against her at Blue Quills Residential School. She never recovered from those experiences.

College changed my life and the lives of the people I shared classes with. We all came as strangers on the first day but at graduation we were in tears saying goodbye to each other. Sault College had an Indigenous Centre called Enji-Maawnjiding that encouraged Indigenous students to gather, study, eat and hold ceremonies. It was a wonderful, comfortable space with computers, couches and a kitchen. Sometimes our classes were taught in the fire arbour outside Enji-Maawnjiding. We would sit around the fire pit and begin our classes with a smudge. I had grown accustomed to it by this point and somehow the smell of the burning sage always grounded and focused me. Just having access to smudge was a comfort, knowing I could go smudge before class or when life was difficult helped a lot. It was like a security blanket, sealing off my body, heart and mind from harm, protecting me with prayer, with the pungent smoke enveloping me.

At times there were conflicts within our groups, but by the end of the second year, we were tight. As I said, twelve of us graduated from the Native Community Worker — Addictions Counsellor Diploma program in 2002.

In the first week of the second year of the program, I was planning my courses with my academic counsellor when all of a sudden I heard screams from inside Enji-Maawnjiding, where the television screens and lounge area were. I ran into the room and saw students staring up at the screens, saying a plane had hit the World Trade Center in New York. People had their hands covering their mouths in shock and some were crying. Most were in disbelief. I went back to see my counsellor thinking that strange things always happen in New York and the United States. A few minutes later I wandered back into the lounge and began watching the screen along with the other students. We all saw the second plane hit the World Trade Center towers. Terror and shock filled my body. A lot of people were crying. The teachers and staff were trying to keep us calm but we felt like the worst thing could happen any moment. My fear was that World War 3 would start or that we would be bombed because we lived on the border of the United States. I couldn't calm down and sobbed, and eventually the Indigenous staff called in an Elder to have a sharing circle for the students who were experiencing shock and trauma. It took a while for me to calm down enough that I could drive home, and once I got there, I couldn't stop watching CNN. I was obsessed with the non-stop reporting and heightened threat of terrorism. This was a moment in history that Westerners will remember forever as shocking and traumatic, to see a plane hit a tower filled with fellow human beings. It wasn't until later in life that I would realize how insidious the politicians were in using that event to declare war in the Middle East, using tactics of fear mongering and Islamophobia.

My biological father Rick came down to Sault Ste. Marie on the Greyhound bus to watch me graduate from college in June 2002. It was a wonderful few days that he was able to stay with me. Rick was amazed that I could drive a car and had my licence because during my time out in Edmonton I was dependent on him for car rides to get groceries or run errands. We went for a ride in the country, to the house I grew up in. We walked around and I shared with him how my sisters and I used to play. I rediscovered our secret forts and the trees we used to climb as young girls. We didn't say much; my dad had a way of talking —like he was thinking about what he was saying. He took his time, forming his sentences deliberately. Our communication styles were very different. I spoke fast and expected an answer right away. Rick spoke evenly and slowly. There were so many times I interrupted him mid-conversation, thinking that he was done speaking, and changed the subject. He would politely answer me, then revert to the first conversation and finish his original thought. I learned to make sure he was finished talking about a subject by giving him a few minutes of silence. Part of me wanted my dad to talk to me about things I longed for, like stories of my sisters and me as children, what kind of baby I was, what his reaction was when I was born, but the words never came out and the answers remained unknown. To this day I haven't asked him those questions. If I do ask him, he may tell me and what if I don't like what he has to say? I would rather not know and pretend that we were wanted, loved and cherished as children before we were taken away. I remember as a child dreaming of a dad who would hug me, kiss my cheek, cuddle, play with me and be so proud of me he would be beaming with pride. He would be my hero, my trusted confidante and best friend. Those dreams faded away as I grew older but now I watch my sons be loving heroes, confidantes and best friends to their daughters and nieces.

During my last three months of college in 2002, our Native Community Worker Addictions Counsellor curriculum required us to fulfill 240 hours of field placement in a social agency. On my own initiative, I called the local women's crisis shelter to see if they would consider taking me on as a student. Women in Crisis was the only women's residential shelter in the city at that time. It offered a safe, secure place for up to thirty women and children fleeing violence. It also offered counselling outpatient services and would accept women who were experiencing homelessness, addictions and/or mental health issues. Working with women and children experiencing crisis was something I knew I could be good at because I had the lived experience as well as training as a counsellor. At this point in my life, I felt ready to help others and was in a good place mentally, physically and emotionally.

I was given an interview with Carol, the supervisor of the women's crisis shelter. My first impression of her was that she made me feel at ease with her approachable manner and eagerness to help me. She asked me some questions about my background, where I saw myself working and my career goals in the next few years. I was given the student placement at that very interview. I was elated and went back to the college to tell my teacher. I was the envy of my class for securing such a prominent placement on my own initiative.

Working at the women's crisis shelter was one of the best jobs I had. Although it was only a student placement, I was exposed to a lot of crisis situations. From March to May of 2002, I went from being a student observer to taking crisis phone calls and dealing with women and children who came to the shelter in crisis, crying and terrified. Being able to comfort them, remain calm and focused, and offer support was something I became skilled at.

My placement ended in May 2002. I wanted to continue working there, so I secured some funding through the local Indian Friendship Centre employment program for out-of-province First Nations students. Once again, my initiative paid off and eventually led to Women in Crisis hiring me permanently. All of my co-workers at the shelter had degrees and at least ten years' seniority in crisis and social work. I was the only one with a diploma, but my lived experience and ability to listen and respond calmly worked in my favour tremendously.

While working at the shelter there were times I was emotionally triggered, where my body felt a memory of the past violence inflicted on me. Sometimes seeing facial bruises, split lips or reading the case files caused me to flinch and squeeze my eyes shut, but I pushed through it and sequestered it in my body — absorbing that emotion, pushing it deep down into my belly to be bottled up. The worst triggering event was seeing a woman experiencing a mental health crisis cut her wrist. It almost caused me to faint at the sight of the blood but I got through it with the help of a co-worker. I was working an overnight shift; there was always only one crisis worker and a household worker doing laundry and cleaning from 11 p.m. to 7 a.m. This middle-aged woman had approached me earlier in my shift to talk. I listened and she spoke about not feeling well. Never at any time did I understand this to mean she wanted to cut herself, nor did I ask if she wanted to harm herself. I had never come across people, in my studies or in life, who self-harmed. After a brief private session with her where she mostly talked about superficial things, she returned to her room. Later that night after the rest of the daytime crisis workers had left, I heard her calling me to the washroom, saying she needed help. When I got to the washroom, she said, "I feel better now" as blood was dripping off her wrists onto the floor.

My first reaction was shock at the amount of blood. I hadn't seen that much blood since I had miscarried years earlier. My second reaction was to try not to pass out or vomit as the saliva in my mouth began to accumulate. In a matter of seconds my heart was racing and my blood felt like it was rushing in my veins. My fight or flight response was in overdrive. It took every ounce of strength to remain calm for the woman as I yelled to my co-worker to call 911. I asked my co-worker to take over with her but I did not explain that it was because the blood terrified me; my job was to respond to crisis, not run from it. After the woman had been whisked away in an ambulance, the executive director came in to debrief with my supervisor because there is a "serious event" protocol to follow when a client self-harms. My insides were still quivering from the adrenaline rush at seeing all that blood. My co-worker said I required more training, which I felt I did too. "Triggered" was not a word in my vocabulary at that time but that is what happened. It took a few days for my body to return to a normal state where I didn't have visions of blood dripping from a wound racing through my mind.

My job at the crisis shelter was fast-paced and as soon as I showed up for work I would be on the floor tending to in-house residents, walk-in clients and crisis phone calls. Sometimes I would literally have to run for the phone or race around to get meds for residents, change bedding or get rooms cleaned and ready for new residents. The shelter was always full and sometimes we had to direct women to another shelter because there was no room left. As I drove to work daily, I would brace myself for events that were out of my control, such as women under the influence, child abuse, stories of sexual and physical abuse. I would pray that I had the strength to deal with it. At the time I believed I was okay but I think now that I really separated myself from my own abuse and locked it away. I must have disassociated from it because I often wondered how I could work with survivors of abuse after having been through so much horrific abuse myself. Before I walked into the shelter I would imagine myself putting on a big, long, magical cloak that would shield me from absorbing the trauma and violence I was exposed to. It worked most of the time.

Shift work was a struggle because I required a babysitter for my kids when I had to leave them at night time. It didn't get any easier when I enrolled in the Bachelor of Social Work degree program at Algoma University. Working full-time shifts and juggling a full course load along with being a single parent was wearing me down. My kids still talk about how they ate take-out every night at Wendy's because mom had to work and didn't have time to cook. All I did was work, study and sleep, and any extra time was spent trying to give the kids some normalcy of life. On those rare occasions we did fun things like swimming, eating out, going to the movies and taking walks along the river. But I couldn't do it much longer because things were starting to fall apart and my grades were suffering.

Being a single parent of three children is a lot of work and the constant struggle to keep food in the house and pay for school field trips, lunches, shoes and clothes was never-ending. I could barely keep up and when I look back, I can't understand how I did it. There are things you just keep on doing no matter what. You drag your ass out of bed or off the couch and you keep going because you have to, because no one is going to do it for you. The fear of having my kids taken away was also a big motivator; I was always afraid Children's Aid would take them away for any little reason.

In 2003 I was contacted out of the blue by Child Welfare in Edmonton. My teenage daughter Naomi had been apprehended from her father Wayne, who had assaulted her. But instead of sending her back to me immediately they had put her in foster care. Wayne had convinced them I was a drunk and a danger to her even though he was the one under investigation. I reluctantly went along with a home study from the Children's Aid Society in Sault Ste. Marie. My supervisor at my workplace, along with many other people who knew me and could vouch for my character, wrote letters of support stating that I was a good parent and employed. Regardless of the letters and the stable environment I was providing for Naomi's younger siblings, CAS refused to place my own daughter in my care. I was furious, threatened to go to the local media and started looking for a lawyer. Within twenty-four hours CAS flew my daughter to Sault Ste. Marie from Edmonton. She had been in foster care for six months during this whole process. She would call me weekly crying on the phone because she wanted to be with us so bad.

Our reunion was emotional. I had not seen Naomi since she was eight years old, when we left Edmonton. What was she like? Did she hate me? We waited at the airport as she disembarked from the small airplane with a social worker. She ran into my arms sobbing. It was very emotional for her siblings also. They grew up knowing they had an older sister but did not know anything about her. She was a beautiful girl with shoulder-length, dark-chocolate-coloured hair, a fair complexion, a heart-shaped face and petite. She was the spitting image of me when I was a teenager. After many years of separation my first-born daughter was finally back in my care.

Naomi was happy to be back with me at first but she was jealous of her siblings — something she openly admitted to and which was totally understandable. Her jealousy came from not being raised with them and feeling like I cared more about them than her. Naomi didn't understand that her younger siblings loved her and looked up to her and were proud to have a big sister. The first few months were hard for both of us because she stayed so close to me and was always in my personal space, grabbing my hands and clinging to me, which jarred my nerves. My younger children never clung to me or grabbed my hands; I would be the one to initiate touch or tenderness. I would push Naomi away out of habit and even cringe from her touch, not because I was repulsed by her but because of my instinctive need to protect my personal space from wandering, molesting hands. I tried very hard not to cringe or pull away and it must have been very confusing for her also. Even as an adult with my own children, I could not break free from the lasting effects of sexual abuse.

The brainwashing by her father Wayne and her stepmother Geraldine, who portrayed me as a drunken Indian welfare mother who did not want her, had lasting impacts. Wayne made sure to plant the seeds of doubt and sickness in my daughter Naomi's mind so that she would always feel her mother abandoned her and would grow to hate me. Our relationship has been tumultuous because I am not only dealing with my own child but a person who was raised by racist, non-Indigenous people who did not support her or encourage her to be proud of being Plains Cree. My daughter tells me that Wayne and Geraldine would fight and argue and then cry on her shoulder. She would mediate between them and gossip to each parent about the other one. We did not do these things in our home or talk negatively about each other.

On one occasion when Naomi was fifteen and we were arguing, she yelled that she hated me and that I had never wanted her, which led me to produce stacks of affidavits and mediation reports to show her that I had tried to regain custody. At one point when she was still with her father, I had written to an MPP in Edmonton to investigate child welfare reports I had made against Wayne because I did not believe they were taking my concerns about Naomi's safety seriously. Naomi read through all the documents but I think it took a while for her to believe that I really did fight for custody of her but the system was not in my favour. To the courts I was what Wayne said I was — an unfit "Native" mother, even though I had three children in my custody and had never been investigated for neglect or abuse.

I have never been under investigation by Child Welfare for neglect or abuse. Nonetheless, the lies and allegations from Naomi's non-Indigenous father were enough for them to keep her from me, showing that in both Alberta and Ontario, the child welfare systems have a racist bias against Indigenous people.

But by 2004 Naomi was back in our household. I had four children and was struggling to work, go to university and raise these kids. It was challenging but also fun. They were creative, happy-go-lucky children who would put on skits for me and listen to music loud while we all danced around the living room. We would go to the movies or for walks along the lakeshore to skip rocks. We did everything together and all my free time was devoted to their happiness and recreation. Unfortunately I did not focus on their schooling too much — I made sure they went to school but I did not value it as many parents do. School was hard for all of them; they experienced a lot of bullying and racism but also struggled with learning. Three of my kids had learning disabilities and Jonathan had also been diagnosed with a slight brain injury.

During the summer of 2004 Cree's behaviour began to change drastically and he became quite aggressive and challenging. He would yell, scream and throw things around. He was angry and constantly challenging my authority. His younger sister and brother were terrified of him and I had no idea what was happening. He would rage and they would hide in their bedrooms. On several occasions I had to call the police because I did not know what else to do. He tore boards off the shed and chased my neighbour with a hammer. Just when I thought it couldn't get any worse, Cree disclosed to me that someone we trusted — a caregiver — had sexually molested him. Naomi was triggered by Cree's disclosure and within twenty-four hours she wrote me a letter and left it on my bed, disclosing that her father had molested her also. It felt like a bombshell went off in my house.

As a survivor of sexual abuse I knew the road ahead would be rough for them. I felt tremendous guilt that my children had experienced sexual abuse and I had been unable to protect them. Our house was in crisis and a series of visits by the police and Children's Aid Society took place. We were asked to go to the Children's Aid office where they recorded statements about the abuse my children experienced. Charges were laid against the perpetrators and then counselling for the kids began. All this happened within a two- or three-week time frame and my memories of it are blurry at best because it was such a whirl-wind of emotions, reports, appointments and making sure the kids were okay. Their abusers were charged; in Cree's case his abuser was charged with six counts of sexual assault, and Naomi's father was charged with two counts of sexual assault.

Fortunately, they were able to get into counselling to support their disclosures. I should have gone to counselling too because my blood pressure and anxiety were high. At the time my thinking was not rational; being in crisis caused reactionary responses that led to decisions I regretted later. Some of those decisions included quitting my job at the women's shelter and my full-time studies at university to focus on supporting my children and providing stability while they went through counselling. My thinking at the time was I didn't deserve to be a crisis worker: I had failed as a parent because I had allowed my children to be sexually abused. It was a rough time for all of us, and it meant giving up my income and living in poverty again. Both Naomi and Cree gave me a difficult time when it came to discipline and setting boundaries in the home. There were many instances of Naomi drinking, drugging and arguing, and I had to go to the school because she had been suspended for fighting. Our home life was tumultuous; she would fight me over every boundary I placed. If I grounded her she would make my life miserable by throwing things at me, writing terrible things in lipstick on the mirror and screaming obscenities at me. I would sit at the bottom of the stairs so she couldn't run out the front door and she would throw a barrage of items at me. Her father had never given her boundaries so she didn't know what it meant to be grounded for misbehaviour.

At this point in my life I was not in a good place to be a calm, collected parent either — I would yell and scream back.

Sometimes we would be in each other's faces, yelling and threatening each other. It was awful. Eventually these violent confrontations led to one bad enough that I kicked her out. She pushed me and I grabbed her, turned around and led her out the front door. After that Naomi went to live with my adoptive mother, who was more than happy to interfere in my parenting and let me know she thought I had failed as a mother.

Things calmed down for a bit in our household but I couldn't shake the feeling that my adoptive mother was undermining my parenting. A few days after Naomi was kicked out, the CAS called me to report that I was being accused of assaulting Naomi. There are no words to explain the rage and betrayal I felt towards my adoptive mother. She had taken the whole situation out of context and made it look like I assaulted Naomi by pushing her out of the house. My visit with CAS was short and they didn't do anything at all except talk to me.

For a long while Naomi would not talk with me or visit me. My adoptive mother had a great influence on her life. To this day I try to understand how a woman who watched my sisters and me be physically and sexually abused by her husband could try to make up for her failures by raising my daughter and my late sister Gina's children.

~~~

I have unresolved rage towards my adoptive mother because I felt she perpetuated harmful talk about my sisters and me. Mary's sisters were condescending and passive-aggressive towards me about anything they felt they could get away with, even going as far as making comments about my weight, how I raised my children, and how my sisters and I were a disappointment and could have done so much by becoming pianists, swimmers or artists. I also have no doubt we could have been amazing if it weren't for the fact that my adoptive father beat the shit out of us, called us names and constantly tried to molest and rape us. Our lives were once full of potential because we were smart, resourceful, athletic and talented. But our self-esteem was weak, our sense of security and stability was not intact and we had neither the emotional support nor the encouragement to do well from our parents. We had been damaged, emotionally and physically scarred by this family. All this is hard to tell my own children because they want so badly to have a family and grandparents to speak about. They don't want to hear that their gramma is a bad person; my daughters were very protective of their gramma at that time.

After a few months Naomi and I began to talk to each other through email and then, eventually, to visit each other. She would come over and spend a night or two — she would sleep in bed with me, we would talk and laugh until late at night. Eventually it came time to testify against her father/ abuser in court. The Provincial Court of Alberta flew us back to Edmonton for a preliminary hearing to see if there was enough evidence to proceed to trial, and although Naomi was terrified, she was also staunch in pursuing legal action against her father, Wayne.

We had a court helper, also named Naomi, who escorted us through the process and made sure we were not alone at any point, to deter Wayne from approaching Naomi. When it was her turn to give testimony, she was shielded behind a screen and didn't have to look at her abuser. After her testimony she had a bloody nose and was greatly affected by what she had to talk about. The courage it took for her to speak out in court with others watching and listening to the horrors she endured while in her father's care was extraordinary. I was not allowed in the courtroom to listen, no reason was given to me, and shortly afterwards we had to fly back to Sault Ste. Marie. On the flight home Naomi seemed catatonic, barely spoke a few words and also refused to eat. I was very concerned that she would not bounce back but after a few days of good rest, she was okay.

We had to return to Edmonton later that year and once again Naomi spoke bravely and forcefully about the violence she experienced at the hands of her father. This time we stayed in a nice little hotel in downtown. The weather was bitter cold once again. We decided to get a bite to eat and headed to the mall closest to our hotel. We never suspected that Wayne would be in that mall, firstly because it was mostly inaccessible by car but also because it was late in the evening. Naomi always worried about her younger step-siblings, especially her younger sister who was also abused and in her stepmother's custody. Geraldine had strict conditions from child welfare authorities meant to protect her children and she was not allowed to have contact with their father, Wayne. Naomi's father had no respect for laws, police or rules — he openly defied any court order and felt above the law. While Naomi and I were shopping, we spotted Wayne with Geraldine and her two younger siblings. They didn't see us so we ducked behind a row of panties in the department store. Naomi was terrified of him and her hands were trembling. We left the mall immediately for fear that we would run into him again. The next morning, just before the court hearing, we told the court worker who promptly told the police, and Geraldine's children were apprehended from her care. Unfortunately the charges were later dismissed because it was Naomi's word against her father's.

As with Naomi's sexual abuse charges, all six charges against Cree's abuser were dismissed; they believed Cree was too young to testify against his abuser. This did not mean his abuser didn't do it, it just meant that the court didn't feel it had a strong enough case to convict. Cree's abuser was registered on the sex offender's list and remains there to this day, unable to get a job working with children.

It is abhorrent that we have a legal system in Canada that tells parents and young people that the legal system works and to report sexual abuse. It does *not* work and in this case, it greatly failed two young people who bravely went on record to talk about their sexual abuse.

That chapter in our lives closed and it was a great disappointment to tell my children that the men who sexually abused them would face no legal consequences.

## CHAPTER 8

# Ekaa naantaw kaa-wiikihk

A S TIME MARCHED ON and the children grew into teenagers, my illusion of having a "normal family life" was fading. I felt like I was barely hanging onto my own sanity and health, and raising teenagers was a new phase and a whole different style of parenting that I had no experience in. Raising teenagers who haven't experienced trauma is hard enough, but coupled with the trauma of sexual abuse, the anger and disappointment they directed at me felt overwhelming. I was barely capable of dealing with it. There were a lot of people telling me what I "should" be doing but none had actually raised four children by themselves.

Guilt and shame drove me to do better, and anger kept the fires stoked. I cannot count the times I fantasized about running away with my children and starting over in a new place. To this day the kids will laugh and joke about the places I've told them we would move to: New Zealand, Baltimore, New York, Toronto and even back to Edmonton as a last resort. I was afraid to tell people about my plans because after a few times they would say, "The kids need stability, and you can't just pick up and leave." But I wanted so badly to just get away from the feelings of inadequacy, to avoid conflict and to avoid confronting my adoptive mother for how I felt about her.

Naomi and Cree were teenagers in grades nine and eleven and getting those two to attend school regularly was a battle. They faced bullying every day, and even though Naomi lived with my adoptive mother, I would still get calls from the school when she was in trouble or when she missed class. Naomi had established herself as a bully of sorts and kids had learned not to mess with her. Her older cousins Cheyenne and Jonah (Gina's kids) had previously attended that school; no one messed with them either. When Naomi found out her brother Cree was being picked on, she confronted the bullies and told them she would kick their asses or get her cousin to do it for her. It was a mess and Cree managed to get himself into a few fights but he did stand up to the bullies. He was not a typical macho boy who was into sports; instead he picked up a guitar and music was his passion. On his sixteenth birthday I bought him a black Cort EVL6 acoustic guitar and from that day onwards he never stopped playing and teaching himself. I thank the Creator for giving him the gift of music as an outlet for all the hurt and pain he experienced as a child and youth.

The two younger children also struggled in school with bullying, especially Jonathan who was the baby among the siblings. Jonathan was diagnosed with a brain injury from birth and also Attention Deficit Disorder (ADD) at the age of six. I was constantly being called to the school because of behaviours they deemed too difficult for the teachers to manage. He was always being sent home for things like wandering around the school, fighting and causing problems with other children. After we were given a referral to see a psychologist, Jonathan had a series of appointments for testing. He did funny things when he was restless to avoid boring activities, and on several occasions during his appointments he would ask to go to the bathroom. This particular bathroom had a shower stall in it and we would hear him in there playing, which caused the psychologist and me to giggle about him pretending to go to the bathroom to escape his boring medical appointments. He was diagnosed with ADD and a slight brain anomaly. Jonathan was given medication for his ADD, he got new glasses and he was put on an adjusted Individual Education Plan (IEP) at school. Even with all these supports in place, school was still difficult for him because he struggled with making friends and had a hard time picking up on verbal/nonverbal communication cues. It was painful as a parent to see his anguish when he was not invited to birthday parties and on one occasion did not receive any Valentine's Day cards. His heart was broken because we had spent the evening before making cards for each of his classmates, and he received none in return. His teacher blamed it on him not being on the class list because he went to the resource room every day.

When I look back on the struggles my children faced in school, I think they were mistreated for many reasons but primarily because they were Indigenous and had learning disabilities. I also taught my children to speak up and speak out in their classes about what the teachers were teaching or about things they were experiencing, and this might have set them apart in some ways. On one occasion Jonathan was sent home with a school project to create a "typical Indian village" for an Aboriginal awareness project, meaning they wanted the stereotypical illusion. I was furious at the school and was going to help him make a project that showed what life in the reserve was really like, complete with a dilapidated house, barrels of water outside, an outhouse and an Indian Agent office. My son didn't like this idea and was mortified that I would even consider telling the truth; he knew his teacher would not like that. In the end we sent back a miniature sweat lodge outside of a house.

On many occasions the kids would come home telling stories of what the teachers said about Native people, and Cree would challenge his teachers constantly about their content or even about their lack of truth. By grade ten, Cree had managed to establish a resource room for Indigenous students because he had been so outspoken about making sure our history was taught accurately in classes. He was very proud of this and so was I.

In 2005, Joseph, Charmaine's father, came back into my life. Over the years I had kept in contact with his mother who lived in Regina, Saskatchewan, and he always knew how to find me because my adoptive mother had a listed phone number. He had sent an urgent message through her so I immediately called his mother. Joseph came to the phone and whispered that his eldest daughter, Trina, was gone. She had committed suicide and I could hear in his voice that getting the words out of his body and past his throat was incredibly painful. He told me Trina's mother had to break into her bedroom through the window because she had barred the door before ending her life. There's no way to prepare for what to say in moments like that, especially through the phone. All I could do was listen, empathize and offer support whenever he needed to talk. For the next few days we would talk for hours on the phone and I supported him while he anguished over why she did it. There were no answers.

Joseph asked if he could come visit for a bit to get away, to which I agreed as long as he remained sober. It had been thirteen years since we'd last seen each other and the child we shared was a teenager. The last image in my mind was a virile, healthy Native guy with long black hair and a killer smile. Three days later he made his way on the Greyhound from Regina to Sault Ste. Marie, and I didn't recognize him when he stepped off the bus. The years of drinking had worn him down, his long hair was sparse and time had bent him over a bit. For a brief minute I wanted to turn around and run, but I didn't. We embraced and headed back to meet the kids. At first it was awkward being together, and the first night in bed he told me the reason he first got together with me back in 1992 was because he was on the run from the Canada-wide warrant and needed a place to stay. He admitted that he fell in love with me after a while but it kind of hurt to know that he had used me back in the day, staying at my place so he wouldn't get caught. My romanticized version of our love story fell apart. I had built it up to be more than it was.

We fell into a comfortable relationship and there were many things we did that he had never done before, like go to the beach or to a movie theatre. Going to the movies was a thing we would do weekly and he would get excited for each new release. Sometimes when we were talking I would ask him about his dreams and he would tell me he had none. There was nothing he dreamt about, no travel destination or goal to work towards. This mystified me and I would push him to draw upon even one dream, but there was nothing. Closer to Christmas he received residential school monies, and he bought the kids some gadgets and new jackets and sent money to his relatives. He also bought a mini-van for us and this was his way of paying back "child support" he owed to me.

Christmas must have been a triggering time for Joseph, with his daughter's passing making it even harder. He told me that everyone in his family partied and drank during the holidays. Sure enough, Christmas Day he took off and drank all day at the bar and then came home drunk and belligerent. We broke up and he took off that night for a hotel. The next day he left on the bus to Regina. After the New Year, he ran out of money, sobered up and took a bus back to Sault Ste. Marie.

Joseph was on the wagon for a while after that. Eventually he found temporary work and then got hired onto an assembly line, which supplemented my income. I was comfortable with him and fell back into a domestic life that felt like two roommates sharing space, going to movies and taking care of each other. The intimacy I craved and needed was missing from our relationship, and talking was non-existent except if it was about the weather, movies, gossip or sports. Nothing intimate, deep, soulful or involving feelings was ever brought up. I was grateful for our friendship and we had many good times but there was no spark; instead I feared he would abandon me at any minute for booze. Anxiety and suspicion took over because I did not trust him, and he spoke of being with other women when he partied, which hurt the most. When Joseph was upset with me, he would ignore me for hours or days and no matter how hard I tried to talk with him, he would give me the silent treatment.

Joseph fell off the wagon two more times and showed up at my work drunk. My clients spoke of drinking and using coke with him, and shame and embarrassment took over my feelings. Determined to fix him, I begged and bargained with him to seek treatment and was relieved when he did. But he went to treatment because I wanted him to quit drinking rather than for his own reasons, and in treatment he collected women's phone numbers and kept in contact with them when I was gone to work. At this point I felt obligated to stay with him and stick it out because he had tried. The feelings and trust were gone for me and talking about it was impossible. We finally parted ways for good in 2008, though it was tough because he would call me repeatedly, drunk and begging to come back. After a while the phone stopped ringing and I was able to close that chapter in my life and never look back. I never wished him harm and I cared about him but I couldn't deal with the alcoholism.

Through all these struggles and confrontations, I would get the urge to run — much like a fight or flight response. I never left but I continued to make imaginary plans to go to faraway places like New Zealand, England or New York. In my personal life I was having difficulty standing up to people I felt were bullies and I was easily intimidated, fearing what the outcome would be if I spoke up about how they treated me. I knew from experience that if I confronted them it would usually escalate to violence or I would retreat in tears. I wasn't taught how to approach difficulty in interpersonal relationships, I just learned from what I had seen and experienced in my own toxic relationships. I stuffed all my anger and fear deep down inside where it grew like a malignant tumour, infecting me with hatred, resentment, sarcasm and self-loathing.

In the past my addictions had helped me cope with these feelings but drugs and alcohol were not an option anymore and smoking had almost killed me. In 2007 I was rushed to the hospital with chest pains, tingly hands and severe dizziness. The doctor told me that after he was done with me I would never want to smoke again, and he was right. Part of the protocol for women with chest pains is a chest x-ray, and dye is given intravenously while you are put into a CAT scan to see if there are blocked arteries. The doctor prescribed me a drug called Plavix, explained a medical procedure in case they found a blockage and said that the probability of having a stroke was high if I kept smoking. This scared me straight. As with things in the past, it took extreme measures for me to quit cold turkey but the thought of my kids growing up without a mother was enough to motivate me. It was the hardest thing I ever did besides giving birth and quitting drinking.

Quitting smoking cold turkey was torture and my days were long, filled with bouts of crying, insomnia, nausea, bargaining, scheming and dreaming of ways to sneak a smoke and not have a stroke. Weeks of severe depression and thoughts of suicide resulted in a trip to the doctor's office and ended with me being prescribed Celexa for depression and Ativan to sleep and relieve anxiety. I felt back to normal in a month or so and had kicked my addiction after twenty-four years of heavy smoking.

In place of smoking I took up eating and gained eighty pounds within two years.

As if raising *two* teenagers wasn't hard enough, there were *two* more to go through the painful years of peer pressure, drug exposure and an attempt at suicide. When my youngest son Jonathan was thirteen years old, I gave him a bit more leeway and privilege to take a bus and hang out with his friends as long as he checked in consistently with me. He had met a new friend and was spending all his free time with this boy. One night at around 10 p.m., the Sault Ste. Marie Police showed up at my door with my son and said they had found him passed out on a bench at the bus station. I was horrified. He did not smell like alcohol and could barely walk but the cops left him with me without saying anything else. His words were slurred and his speech didn't make sense at all. By this time Jonathan's older brother Cree had showed up. We sat Jonathan down to ask questions, and he stated he had taken a bunch of pills with his friends. They had ingested sixteen cold and flu tablets. This was the first time Jonathan had used drugs to get high. We rushed him to the hospital and upon arriving they took him to the cardiac room. His heart rate and blood pressure were dangerously high and my worst fear had come true. Seeing nurses rushing around and my kid being hooked to cardiogram machines scared the shit out of me. By this point Jonathan, who had been hallucinating and talking nonsense, started to cry and reach out to me saying, "Mommy, Mom, I don't want to die!" It took all my willpower to stay calm for him and soothe him because I was terrified too. I held his hand and explained to him that he wasn't going to die and the machines and nurses were helping him. He remained in the hospital for the night under observation until his heart rate slowed down. The nurse told him how lucky he was, that the other kids had been hospitalized also but were very sick. She said these kids were always coming in for overdosing and being drunk. This broke my heart. These were First Nations foster kids and as we passed their rooms we saw their youth workers sitting with them. Jonathan didn't want to see them for a while and that experience scared him straight. He swore he would never do drugs again. That morning I thanked the Creator, cried, and put some tobacco down for those kids.

Naomi had recently graduated from high school and moved to Toronto to live with her stepmother and siblings. It was hard to put her on a bus and watch her leave but it was what she wanted and I let her go. She remained in touch over the summer and came back in the fall, having found life in the big city expensive and her stepmother living in extreme poverty. Naomi and I struggled with communication; we had inadequate interpersonal skills for resolving conflict. We bumped heads constantly and would go long periods without speaking, which made me feel like a failure as a mother.

I had taken a night shift job working as a residential support/crisis line worker in a transitional home for men with severe mental illness, mainly schizophrenia. The residents were kind, talkative and most went to bed sedated on medications so I barely heard a peep throughout the night. My shift was 8 p.m. to 8 a.m. and it was gruelling. Sometimes there would be no phone calls and little to do besides security checks and a few chores, which I usually got out of the way in case a long crisis call came in. The night shift was wreaking havoc on my health and especially my blood pressure. My kids were old enough to stay at home by themselves but I barely got to see them because it was either sleep or work that took priority. I decided to go back to school in the fall and registered again in the Bachelor of Social Work for September 2010.

As my vices were being stripped away, the tremendous confusion and loss of self-identity I was going through became more unbearable. On the surface my life looked okay but I was barely managing. I felt like a drone performing duties because I had no choice. There was no joy, happiness or purpose in my life and the constant crisis after crisis wore my spirit down. I didn't understand where I belonged and felt that my adoptive family was not really my family. In fact I grew to despise them and how they talked about my sisters and how I raised my children. I believed they didn't and shouldn't have anything to say considering their atrocious crimes of neglect, turning a blind eye to the abuse my sisters and I had suffered as children. Stuffing those feelings of resentment made things worse, and as the urge to run grew I began to make plans to leave. I started looking at rental ads for Toronto, Peterborough and even New York because I was determined to escape the Soo.

I continued my studies at Algoma University in the Bachelor of Social Work program but changed all my courses to things I was interested in: Forensics, The History of Music and Anishinaabe Homelands with Eddie Benton Benai. The Forensics class was interesting and brought out this keen desire to change my focus to Forensic Studies and especially homicide. The intricate tasks of collecting evidence and paying attention to detail mixed with the fascination of biology pushed me to apply to Trent University's Forensic Sciences program. I had passed the class at Algoma with a high grade but this was just a basic class, barely scratching the surface. Nevertheless I applied to Trent University, with plans to relocate to Peterborough if my application was accepted. In the back of my mind I knew all too well that I needed a solid foundation in biology and math to be accepted in the Forensics program, but I figured that if they accepted me I would work my ass off to maintain my grades. This was also a way out of Sault Ste. Marie and my kids were willing to move along with me. My adoptive family on Ronald's side lives in Peterborough and wanted to be in my life, and my childhood friend had also moved there, so it seemed to be all falling into place.

By this time Naomi had a boyfriend and was in her ninth month of pregnancy and big as a house. The idea of being a grandmother made me excited but terrified. I thought I was too young to be a grandmother, only thirty-nine years old at the time. On January 8, 2011, Natalie entered our lives. Words cannot describe the exhilarating feelings that went through my body and the instant love I felt for this tiny human being. In the first hour, every time I looked at her I saw myself, my dad, her great-great *kokum* and her mother as a baby. When she came out of her mother, I watched like an eagle as they cut the cord, cleaned her off, and then put her under a heat lamp while they cleared her airway of mucous. She cried with all her might and her little fists clenched as if she was protesting her own birth. Tears of joy streamed down my face. Naomi had been given an epidural so she could not hold Natalie right away and could not see her because of her limited view from the operating table. Naomi kept asking me, "Mom, is she okay?" I said, "Yes, my girl, she is perfect. Perfect." It was then she was put on a scale, measured, cleaned, swaddled and handed to me to show Naomi as she lay waiting for the doctor to deliver her placenta. This was the most overwhelmingly exquisite moment of my life, watching my daughter turn into a mother, and my heart was bursting with pride.

Naomi named her daughter Natalie Cardinal. As the nurses helped clean up Naomi, Natalie was tucked into my arms. As I rocked her, I whispered into her ear, telling her how long we had been waiting to meet her and that I was her *kokum*. The love I felt for this human was unlike anything I had felt in my life. It was different from when my own children were born. Not only did I feel protective of her but like a piece of my heart and soul and our ancestors were in this little human. She was like a gift from the Creator. Naomi's body was reacting to the incredible stress of giving birth and she was vomiting and shaking from shock. It took a while to get her stabilized enough to hold her child for the first time, and it was an amazing time for our family. Being a grandmother seemed to have erased all the sorrow and hope had come to breathe new life into our family. There was a new generation to start over and carry on and we could not mess this up.

A few things happened to set in motion my departure from Sault Ste. Marie and my choice of Ottawa as a destination. Natalie had test results that came back as abnormal and she needed to have further tests done at Toronto's Sick Kids Hospital. Tests showed she might develop cystic fibrosis and they needed to explore with more conclusive tests. The Northern Travel Allowance would only pay for Naomi and the baby but Naomi insisted that I go with her. Through donations raised at the university we collected enough money so I could be in Toronto with her, but we had to travel separately and would arrive within an hour of each other at the same hotel. Naomi was terrified to travel by herself with the baby but she did it and I was proud of her.

That evening we left the hotel to go for a walk around downtown Toronto on Yonge Street. People were everywhere on the sidewalks and we tried to peek into every store with its numerous trinkets and treasures displayed in the windows. Every few stores there would be a restaurant filled with people eating, talking and laughing. I wanted to go sit at the table with them and eat, talk and laugh as well. The love of the hustle and bustle crept back into my veins — I liked the big city. Sault Ste. Marie was nothing like this and mostly consisted of white French or Italian settlers who had little tolerance for Indigenous people and people of colour. A few years back I had visited Washington, DC, for a work conference and at that time remembered that I loved the vibe of a busy city. What struck me as most appealing was the diversity of skin colours and cultures mixed together. The bright lights and non-stop activity felt comforting to me and strangely enough reminded me of where I spent my young adult life in Edmonton. It made me feel alive, excited and in the world! It was that trip that planted the idea of leaving Sault Ste. Marie as soon as I could.

The next day, after our appointment at Sick Kids Hospital for Natalie, we headed back to Sault Ste. Marie. The test results showed Natalie was a carrier of cystic fibrosis and could pass it on to her children but she was no longer in danger of developing it herself. Shortly after this trip Naomi and I had a disagreement and she distanced herself from me. I had set a boundary with her after she had been staying on my couch for weeks and refused to go back to her own furnished apartment. She was angry with me for a long time for asking her to go home but her sleeping on my couch with the baby was not healthy. Her apartment was less than a block away.

Depression set in. I had been diagnosed with clinical depression years earlier, and my symptoms were mostly managed by medication but lately I felt no joy. I had nothing to look forward to, no hope and I felt like I wanted to disappear or die. Dealing with conflict in my life was never easy. If there were any interpersonal conflicts, I ignored them or ceased communication altogether. Instead of fighting, flight was my coping mechanism — run, run, run. My plans to leave Sault Ste. Marie were still in motion and in my personal love life, I had begun to talk online with a man, Earl, who lived in Ottawa. He was aware that my plan was to move to Peterborough and attend Trent University. Earl and I talked every day on webcam for three months and then one day a letter came in from Trent University explaining that I had not been accepted into the Forensic Sciences program. My heart was crushed and I felt like lashing out; rejection was a hard pill to swallow.

During this time, I had gotten into a disagreement with two of my childhood friends and we were not talking anymore. These women were well educated, stable and had been my backbone; they had kept me in line when I wanted to run over the years. They were aunties to my kids and we had grown up together, but racism and settler colonialism were the straws that broke the camel's back. Their disagreement was unsettling for all involved and had to do with racism within our "family of choice." No one in our family wanted to talk about settler colonialism, and in fact I only had a vague idea of what it was. At this point in my life "colonialism" was not part of my vocabulary and calling settlers "settlers" seemed very rude, or so a settler told me. All this turmoil, coupled with the need to run, was enough ammunition to fuel my getaway.

My online relationship had taken a turn and Earl had invited me to come stay with him and his kids in Ottawa. This sounded appealing to me because he was a single father of two teenagers and was offering somewhere to go. Common sense would dictate that you don't drop everything in your life, sell all your belongings and run away to live with a perfect stranger, but my head wasn't in the right place. Even if someone had tried to convince me to stay, or to venture out on my own, I would not have listened. I was stubborn and had convinced myself that if I could just get to Ottawa, I would come up with a plan. I always did. My overwhelming urge to escape Sault Ste. Marie caused me to withdraw into myself. Instead of seeking help from others to cope with the turmoil in my life, I chose to run.

Jonathan was only sixteen at the time, so he came with me to Ottawa. Cree, who was eighteen, chose to stay behind with his friends because he didn't want to move yet, and Charmaine lived with her gramma. Naomi was still not talking to me or allowing me to see the baby. My time in Sault Ste. Marie was done. I felt like I had nothing left and if I didn't go, I would kill myself. I had never been able to deal with conflict; when confronted, I would either leave or become aggressive and abusive. I could not work up the nerve to confront my family of choice about our recent conflicts, which had left us not talking to each other. I bottled everything up and used my pent-up anger and resentment to hurl my kids and myself into the unknown: a move to Ottawa.

I sold my valuable belongings within a week and donated my extra clothes and knick-knacks; the rest I packed in totes and put in storage. My plan was to leave on the next payday and I had handed in my notice to quit work two weeks prior. I told a few people but decided to wait until the last minute to tell others so they wouldn't try to convince me to stay. I wanted them to all fuck off with their holier-than-thou speeches, guilt trips, talk of "family obligation" and comments about how irresponsible I was being. Self-preservation took over. My son was not as motivated as I was to leave; he expressed that he didn't want to go without his brother. Cree promised he would join us later and Jonathan reluctantly came with me because there was no one to take care of him. I went to say goodbye to Naomi and the baby, but things were tense between us still and I knew she was mad at me for leaving. It wasn't until I wrote this story out that I admitted that if there had been somewhere for Jonathan to stay, I would have left him behind too, to run, run, run. It makes me sad and ashamed to admit this.

We boarded the Greyhound bus on May 13, 2011, with a duffel bag and a suitcase full of our belongings. Some of Jonathan's friends came to say goodbye. He was very sad and wouldn't speak to me very much on the bus ride. I knew it hurt him to say goodbye to his friends and to the only place he had known as a child. The bus ride was long and Jonathan sat behind me, grumbling and complaining. I didn't blame him, I knew it was hard for him to leave his friends. We arrived in Ottawa the next day, Earl waiting for us at the bus station. He wasn't very friendly and tapped my shoulder, gave me a feeble hug and ushered us into a waiting cab. We barely spoke and I could see my son had tears in his eyes. He was really hurting and scared so I told him things were going to be okay and I could make things right. Earl sternly said, "Why you crying?" This was my first inkling that I wouldn't like the way he talked to my son.

Earl's apartment was in the west end of Ottawa, on the eleventh floor of a highrise. His children were there to greet us. They were teenagers, extremely polite and obedient, but what caught my attention was that their gaze never met their father's face or eyes. When he spoke to them they either looked away or at the ground, which was unnerving to see. He ordered his daughter to make some food for us, to which she replied that there was none. So with the remaining money left in my bank account, we took a walk to get some groceries. I had a bad feeling. My instincts told me this was not a good place to be and we might need to go to a shelter. Jonathan went with the teenagers that day to go look around downtown Ottawa. They showed him which bus to take to get downtown. Earl asked me how much money I had and when he said he wanted me to put insurance on his car, warning bells started going off in my head. Things were not like we had talked about. I told him I wanted to leave and texted my son's cell phone to tell him to come back so we could pack up and leave. Using my cell phone I searched online for women's shelters and Indigenous women's shelters. I called one of them and they told me how to get to their shelter, which was very far from where we were in west Ottawa. As we tried to leave with our belongings, Earl blocked the door and then told his kids I didn't like them. He refused to let me leave and tried to guilt me into staying but we kept pushing past him.

Earl followed us down in the elevator and when we reached the main floor, his landlord was in the lobby. He proceeded to tell her that I was leaving him, that we didn't want him. It was terribly embarrassing and scary at the same time. He followed us out onto the road and to the bus stop, but thankfully the bus came right away and we were able to get away from him. Calling the police was not an option at this point because I was so embarrassed for meeting someone online and thinking it would be a safe situation. Even in our crisis we looked out the windows and admired the beautiful scenery and landscape on our twenty-minute ride to downtown Ottawa.

When we reached the transit stop called Mackenzie King, we exited the bus. All we had were some basic instructions on how to get to the shelter and no sense of which way to head. Jonathan wanted a smoke but we had no idea where to find a store either, so we started to walk. With all the luggage, it was a gruelling walk. We passed city hall, lots of tall buildings, and we walked seven blocks west without realizing we had gone the wrong way. We were exhausted and emotional, and I kept apologizing to Jonathan who was lashing out at me in anger and because he wanted a cigarette. Poor kid, this was overwhelming for him — shame and guilt boiled in my belly. We had no idea where we were and my cell phone was dead so we had to ask for change from someone on the street, which was humiliating. Flashes of me panhandling crossed my mind. I squeezed my eyes shut to block it out. I called the shelter to explain we were lost, hungry and tired so they sent a Salvation Army van to pick us up. We had walked in total fourteen blocks the wrong way. The shelter was for Native women and their children and the worker was friendly and greeted us kindly. As soon as we got into the door of the shelter, Jonathan broke down in tears. As I comforted him, I ended up crying also. It was an emotional experience and he kept saying, "I can't believe we are homeless." Guilt flared in my gut, shame caused my cheeks to burn. I wanted to die. It took a while to get Jonathan grounded and to stop crying; it was too much for him. After a tour of the shelter house we got settled into our room. Our intake process was long as I explained the online relationship ordeal and that we could not return to Sault Ste. Marie, which it seemed they were trying to arrange for us. I was adamant about staying in Ottawa, though Jonathan protested. He didn't understand that I was running from my problems, how could he? I had decided that he would not go back to Sault Ste. Marie to live so long as he was my dependent, which was very controlling and selfish of me as a mother. Of course I wasn't thinking rationally and was in survival mode, plotting my next moves and always strategizing "what if" scenarios. If you have never been in survival mode and cannot relate, it's like being in a constant state of crisis, ready to react. This is exhausting for the body and mind, but I had little insight into this while I was going through it.

Jonathan and my other children had never lived in a shelter or any other institution and were used to being provided for by me exclusively. They were used to mom cooking, cleaning, buying, making the rules, enforcing the rules and always being tough, rigid and never weak. It must have been very scary for my children to see me so vulnerable and in a different state. I wasn't going to be there with open arms after school, offering cookies and milk, taking them on an adventure to skip rocks by the waterfront, going to the movies or playing any of the typical mom roles.

Jonathan and I shared a room at the shelter. We had bunk beds across from each other and he immediately put up a sheet to have some privacy. As for me, I began using the journal the intake worker had given me to record my feelings and thoughts. My reflections during that time were hopeful about creating a new life but they were also full of guilt and shame for causing a crisis for my children. During those first few months in the shelter and out in the community, I would constantly ask Jonathan if he was okay and he would snap back, "I'm fine," then it would be "Shut up, I'm tired of you asking me if I'm all right." Sometimes I would try to start up a conversation with him and he would tell me I talked too much or he would walk ahead of me to avoid chatter. I was amused and knew that if he was replying to me, angry or not, at least he was talking. I never chastised him for these little bursts of anger because it was his way of acting out towards me to show his displeasure at living in Ottawa, and I believed I deserved it. He had to admit that he did like it at some point and that it was better than Sault Ste. Marie.

But it didn't take long before Jonathan and I had a breakdown. I was still dealing with some serious unresolved mental health and trauma issues. I immediately threw myself into finding employment and secured a job interview right away as a mental health worker. I did well during the interview but because I had no experience facilitating a workshop, I was passed over. Even as I went through the interview process, I doubted whether I was able to do mental health work. I was so fucked up at this point and was in no position to be helping others. It was probably a stroke of luck for the clients that I wasn't hired at this time. The tremendous stress and dire situation of being homeless, in crisis and running from my own problems were taking their toll. I was no longer able to be an effective, empathetic crisis worker.

Two things happened to me that changed the direction of my life and set me on a new course of healing and change within. The first event was Jonathan and me getting into an argument about living in a shelter in poverty. Our income went to zero immediately. Jonathan was not used to having nothing and sharing his space with twenty other people. It was so hard on him; this was the lowest point in our lives. The workers took us aside so that we could resolve our disagreement in a private room. Jonathan really let me have it. He told me how bad a mother I was, how I had messed up his life. The workers were trying to convince me to take him back to Sault Ste. Marie. I got up and walked out of the shelter and walked until I couldn't walk anymore. I wanted to die. I figured if I left Jonathan there at least he would be cared for and they would find him a good home. He didn't deserve what I had put him through and neither did the other kids. Guilt and shame were driving me to come up with a suicide plan. I didn't have any idea of how to do it, I just wanted not to wake up anymore with these painful feelings. My mind would race with thoughts of, "How do you kill yourself without pain?" I certainly wasn't thinking of how it would hurt anyone, all I cared about was stopping the pain of feeling guilty, ashamed and sad. I always felt like no one acknowledged my hurt; I brushed it aside to be a parent, to be responsible, to work, to provide, and it had finally overflowed to the point where I could not hide or stuff it anymore. I had hit rock bottom.

As I sat on the riverside on the bench crying my eyes out, my cell phone rang. It was a childhood friend. I'd given the shelter her number as a person to contact in case of emergency and I guess this was an emergency. The shelter worker had told them I had abandoned Jonathan at the shelter. I whispered into the phone to her that I wanted to die, but she firmly instructed over the phone, "Get up off the bench and walk back to the shelter because Jonathan needs you," and so I did. And I thank her for doing that because I really needed to hear that. I apologized to the staff and also to Jonathan and hugged him so tight. We came up with a plan to send him to Peterborough to stay with some cousins so he could escape the shelter environment for a while.

The second event was an encounter with an animal in

the most unexpected place. I had just put Jonathan on a Greyhound bus to Peterborough and had nothing else to do because I didn't know a single soul in Ottawa. I decided to take a bus ride to where there was a big pow wow in downtown Ottawa. As I was sitting at the bus stop close to the shelter, I felt a gentle gush of wind behind me, ruffling my clothes. I turned and looked over my right shoulder and then my left shoulder. I saw the white tail end of a small deer bounding away from me towards the park area about a block behind the bus stop. This was unreal, an encounter with a deer in downtown Ottawa on a hot May afternoon around three in the afternoon. I immediately stood up and went in the direction of the deer because it had happened so fast that I needed to confirm it had really happened.

No one else had seen the deer and I sat in shock because I knew deer didn't come running through the city. I carried this feeling with me all day and talked about it with a friend who told me to put down tobacco. This animal coming to me meant something but I didn't know at the time how significant it was. I was instructed to put tobacco down and later learned that the deer was a teaching of gentleness and kindness, something I had been denying myself and others. I believe this animal came to me at a time when I needed those teachings of gentleness and kindness in my life, I needed to forgive myself and others, and I needed to heal so I could extend that kindness and gentleness to others, especially my children, who bore the brunt of the hardness of my life.

The hardest part of living in a shelter environment is dealing with other people who are also in crisis with their children. We lash out, our children lash out, and it can be a toxic, scary environment if there aren't residential crisis workers to minimize the impacts of violent outbursts by some of the residents. I give tons of respect to those shelter workers for keeping their heads cool and helping my family during our six-month stay at that shelter.

By the end of August my daughter Charmaine, the second youngest, had moved to Ottawa and into the shelter with Jonathan and me. Cree followed her a few weeks afterward — he ended up going to a young men's shelter. This was a huge adjustment for them and I had to steel myself for the anger, frustration and sadness they would experience starting over in a new city ten times bigger than Sault Ste. Marie. They were sad, withdrawn and sullen at times, never forgetting to remind me how I messed up their lives, how much they missed their friends and how crazy I was.

In the shelter the three of us were sharing one small room. This was challenging because they were my two youngest and they had argued with each other incessantly since they were small children. They fought about the most asinine things, like the TV remote control, computer time and who was the better child. Charmaine thought she was more responsible, wiser and nicer, and she believed it was her duty to chastise her brother at any chance she could. Charmaine did not believe Jonathan had a learning disability or brain injury and felt I treated him better than her and had different, slacker rules for him. Jonathan thought Charmaine was the worst sister in the world, mean and always picking on him. He had no insight into having a disability so he would get angry when his sister pointed out that as much as she teased him about his disability, she also didn't believe he deserved any special parenting.

One day they began arguing and insulting each other in the shelter kitchen. Jonathan reached out and hit Charmaine across the top of the head, which caused her to break out in tears. This was the first time he had ever reacted with physical violence to his sister's bullying. The shelter worker immediately tried to find out what had happened. I described the incident and the shelter worker told Jonathan he had to leave. He took off running out the door because he was afraid they would call the police. He was fifteen years old and on his own in downtown Ottawa. I was going out of my mind trying to figure out what to do, but Cree was able to locate him and convince him to come back. The shelter had arranged for Jonathan to go to a group home because he had been violent. A cloud of gloom hung over my head. I anguished over what had happened and felt so much guilt and shame and was sick to my stomach that Jonathan was in foster care. This all happened over Thanksgiving weekend and when the housing support worker came back on Tuesday, she was shocked to hear Jonathan was gone to foster care. She immediately called the group home and got him back to the shelter. We had to work it out as a family; the kids had to talk about their fighting and how they treated each other. After that incident they were more considerate of each other. Charmaine had to think about how she talked to her brother but he also had to recognize that he could not hit people when he was angry and react to violence with violence.

Our time in that shelter was the most challenging period for all of us. In some ways it brought us closer but it also showed how damaged my family was because of the trauma I had created in their young lives. I look back on these times and cringe because nothing can change what happened yet the guilt of what I did to my children still lingers. My thoughts always go to how I could have done things differently.

~~~

Life played itself out as it needed to, and forgiving myself came with time. The children are young adults now with their own children and they have come to understand that what I did was for my self-preservation, even though it seemed selfish at the time. Coming full circle in my healing as a 60s Scoop

survivor has given me insight into how much of my life I've
spent performing as a "white person": doing what I thought was
acceptable so I'd fit in, trying not to make waves, letting people
walk all over me while the resentment built up inside of me.
From my earliest memory in school, I wanted blonde hair, blue
eyes, to be skinny, popular and accepted. For most of my life I
hated my beautiful brown skin, my gorgeous thick black hair,
my dark-chocolate-brown eyes and even my high cheekbones.
There was no one in my life who looked like me, no one to tell
me my Cree cheekbones were the envy of women who spent
so much money trying to achieve the chiselled look that I had
naturally. My parents didn't say "your skin is so beautiful," but
as an adult I came to realize white women spend hundreds,
even thousands, on sun tanning products trying to achieve the
skin colour that came naturally to me. I inherited my gorgeous
brown colour from my ancestors who have lived on this land
since time immemorial.

All those years wasted hating myself had taken a toll. It
required a great deal of reprogramming to undo the brainwashing, to repair the harm to my psyche. When people ask me what
I did to heal — essentially this meant undoing the harm of the
state trying to assimilate me, to turn me into a non-Indigenous
mainstream Canadian. Up until this point in my life I was still
trying to perform as a white women with brown skin. My life
took a pivotal turn into critically questioning my values, my
belief system and how it affected my thinking. How had my
adoption and experiences of being raised in a non-Indigenous
household, growing up surrounded by non-Indigenous people,
shaped me? How had they affected my views of Indigenous
people, of myself as an Indigenous woman, and of the difficul-
ties I had faced, including formidable obstacles like addictions,
racism, violence and the death of my sister?

I had not realized until then how much internalized racism

had contributed to my identity crisis. This drove me to continue my healing but with a more intellectual understanding of what "identity crisis" and "loss of culture" really meant for 60s Scoop adoptees. I began to understand how loss of identity as Indigenous people had benefitted the state and how easily it gained access to our land and resources. When assimilated Indigenous people become consumed with being "Canadians" and performing as mainstream consumers, they no longer care about their lands, their people or their languages. Our languages teach us how to take care of the land and ourselves. They are essential to our identities as Indigenous people. If we don't reclaim our culture, relearn our languages and practice our ceremonies, we are complicit with the state.

# CHAPTER 9

## Naahta-wiikewin

T HE BEST DECISION I made was signing up for therapy. I went looking for therapy the day after I thought about killing myself at the shelter, during my argument with Jonathan. Counselling in the past had been about me sitting down talking about things that happened to me in the past and sometimes I would struggle to find things to talk about. It was never about how it made me feel or how it affected my mental health and my body. I was skeptical of finding a good therapist. In the past counsellors had never really worked hard at pulling information out of me, which left me feeling like counselling didn't work. This time when I looked for counselling, I wanted someone who knew about the 60s Scoop and could also handle me talking about all the abuse I had experienced. I had once tried to tell someone my story and she told me to stop, that my experiences were traumatizing her and it was too painful for her to listen to. She had been a close friend so I chalked it up to her not wanting to hear how I had been repeatedly assaulted throughout my life. Another time, back in its early stages, I had shown someone the manuscript for this book and they told me they could not read it, it was too traumatic. I began to think no one would be able to listen to my experiences without being traumatized.

I decided that this time I would test the new therapist and ask her if she'd heard stories of physical assault, sexual violence, incest and even murder. Would she be able to listen to me talk about it without trying to shut me down?

Well, my new therapist assured me she had heard everything and I would be safe. She was an older white woman with a welcoming demeanor and kind eyes; she could have been the typical gramma who baked cookies on the weekend for her grandchildren. She was patient and made me feel safe, which was important to me. Being hyper-vigilant helped me analyze people's body language, eye movements and slight changes in facial expressions. As I carefully laid out my story, I watched my therapist for signs of discomfort, disgust, disapproval and even boredom. After a few sessions of laying out my history and what led me to Ottawa, we began to work on undoing some of the emotional turmoil my body was holding onto. The anger and grief within my body frightened me — I had held onto so much of it over the years and now it came rushing out. I sobbed uncontrollably, violently punching the office pillows and lashing out with all the anger I couldn't show as a child, the frustration of being trapped in a household with family members who treated me so terribly. The pillow became my adoptive father's face and I smashed the hell out of it — I swear I would have killed him if the pillow had really been his face. Each punch was for all the times he hit, spanked, kicked, fondled and forced me to do things against my will. The rage coming out scared me but also exhilarated me! I raged against the pillow and let it all out until no more tears came and my arms fell to my sides from exhaustion. For once I had a safe place to vent all the rage without feeling guilty or ashamed. After several sessions and re-enacted scenarios of trauma, the therapist would ground me safely and gently, and I would leave feeling exhausted yet lighter. My therapist was giving me insight into certain behaviours that I had felt ashamed of for many years, like the head banging, sexual promiscuity, trichotillomania (skin picking) and was helping me to understand these behaviours as coping mechanisms to deal with stress, anxiety, trauma and loneliness.

After several months the therapist introduced EMDR (Eye Movement Desensitization and Reprocessing) to our session. She wanted to see if it would help alleviate the stress and anxiety that was causing me to pick the skin on my scalp, leaving behind a bloody mess. I was beginning to lose my hair and people could notice the scabs on my head, so I would wear a hat to hide it. Sometimes I didn't realize this behaviour and would subconsciously daydream, picking and picking until something would snap me back into reality. Some of the things I stressed about were out of my control, and ruminating over worst-case scenarios took up a lot of time. There were triggers — like worry or anxiety about money — that would cause me to pick my skin as a coping mechanism. EMDR sounded scary just by the wording but I agreed to try it. My first session was brief yet we created this lovely safe place that I could retreat to if things got to be too much during therapy. Grounding and leaving the session feeling safe were imperative. Some days I would be exhausted from crying, other days I felt exhilarated, like I was walking on air.

This lovely safe place my therapist and I created was based on a camping spot my sisters and I went to with some of our summer camp friends when we were teenagers. Our parents let us take the canoes out by ourselves. We'd pack two tents, our sleeping bags and some food in a cooler and spend a week out in the bush by ourselves. We pitched our own tents and cooked our own food but the best parts were the campfires, waking up to go swimming, lying on the grass under the stars and listening to the water lapping on the shore. These were the smells, sounds and memories of comfort and safety that would ground me back to my safe space while doing therapy. The therapist and I worked to recreate this place: I would close my eyes, imagine sitting in the cool grass, feel the warmth of the fire, listen to the hissing and crackling of the fire, smell the wood burning. Faintly in the background I could hear the water lapping the shore and recapture that feeling from so long ago, when I was a youth. My body would let go and I would feel safe. These sessions changed me and helped me ground myself when anxiety came.

After many weeks of therapy I decided to take a break and work on employment.

~~~

Finding work was not a problem for me but finding work that I would enjoy was another question. I had done everything from washing dishes, cooking and cleaning to hospital food service and crisis work, and I felt I needed something less stressful. I took a job as a receptionist at the Assembly of First Nations (AFN) and happily settled into what seemed to be a good fit. I was not used to sitting at a desk for eight hours a day so this proved to be my biggest challenge. My second challenge was that some of the people calling were very verbally abusive and would say racist things because it was a national Indigenous organization with a 1-800 number anyone could call toll-free. Some people would call and vent about things they'd seen on the national news about Indigenous people. They would complain, rant and suggest things that we "should" do to make things better for ourselves. They had very little understanding of the systemic issues in regard to Indigenous people. I had one call from a woman in Australia claiming to be Pocahontas reincarnated and insisting she was not portrayed properly in the movie. Although this was an amusing distraction from the typical angry phone calls, there was a huge gap between what people understood about the making of Canada and the true Indigenous history of this country. I got along well with the other staff members, who were pleasant and friendly. The biggest challenge for me was the abusive phone calls, which would set off my anxiety and fear that someone might hate the AFN so much they would cause us harm.

This was very a different kind of work for me, often boring and monotonous, but it was all I could manage at the time. The months flew by. I was trying to find a place for myself but still felt like I didn't fit in. Many things were happening in the Indigenous community and they were impacting our local AFN office. Every day it was something new, the media was always stirring up new stories and the tension was palpable. Answering the telephone was like Russian roulette — anyone could call with the most abusive rants and I'd have to sit there and take it. If I hung up they would call back repeatedly until it went to voicemail and they would leave abusive messages. I felt trapped in an abusive relationship again.

The final straw for me was coming to work on the city bus and feeling dread as I got closer and closer to our office. It was December 2012 and the AFN had been in the national news for weeks for its support of Chief Theresa Spence's hunger strike, and now the Chiefs were supposed to meet with the Prime Minister. I couldn't have cared less about the logistics and didn't get involved in the politics of it. I was to remain non-partisan as an employee. That day of the big meeting, I showed up at work to find security guards at the front door and the elevators on lockdown. The only way up or down was through the guards. They had also stationed a guard by my desk so I was trapped there. Everyone else was locked behind doors that could only be opened with a swipe card, yet as the receptionist I had to remain in the wide-open lobby with only a security guard for protection. I was terrified that something terrible would happen. That feeling remained with me every day after that. I was scared to go to work for fear that someone was out to harm the staff at AFN. I lasted a few more months at AFN but every day got worse. I broke out in the worst case of psoriasis I had ever had. My skin would bleed and one time I bled on an important document on my desk. I did my best to clean it up but I was coming apart at the seams, and when an angry caller reduced me to tears, I finally went to my human resources team. They offered their support and crisis training, and I asked if they could help me handle abusive, racist callers. I had left crisis work so I could be in a less stressful job, thinking receptionist would be a good fit. This was turning into a nightmare for me.

Things got so bad that I requested some time off from work to take care of what seemed to be a crisis and mental breakdown. My skin was so bad that 90 percent of my body was covered in red, angry psoriasis scales that bled if scratched, and scratching was my only relief. I saw a dermatologist who prescribed Methotrexate, a powerful systemic drug that weakens your immune system to stop the rate of cell growth for certain diseases like cancer and psoriasis. This drug made me feel like I had the flu every day; eventually I went to the ER thinking I was very sick. I was told to stop taking the Methotrexate even though my skin was not getting better. Eventually I was referred for UVB light therapy, which was a treatment that you can only get for the most severe forms of psoriasis. The process lasted thirteen seconds at each session. I was required to be completely naked, standing in an upright tube surrounded by lights so strong that I needed to wear special sunglasses. It took longer to take my clothes off and lather skin cream on than it did for the actual light therapy. Afterwards I swear my skin smelled burnt and the nurses had instructed me to stay out of the sun and not to scratch if it felt itchy. This was the skin healing. The treatment worked and after a few months the psoriasis went into remission.

There is nothing more frustrating than people not taking your health concerns seriously or dismissing pain as imagined, expected or weight related. I would be told to lower the stress in my life, eat better, exercise, lose weight, sleep more, do less, and last but not least, "take care of myself." I got to the point where I would search online for "how to take care of yourself." I began to see the same therapist I had been to in the past; she was helping me fill out my insurance papers so that I could get my short-term disability benefits through work. I found out then that she suspected I was struggling with Post Traumatic Stress Disorder (PTSD). For the first time in my life I had an explanation for my "fight or flight" response: the rage, suicidal thoughts, problems with interpersonal relationships, black and white thinking and hyper-vigilance that I could never shut off. My therapist brought me in to do an assessment of the impacts of different violent or traumatic events in my past. The scale measured how severe and traumatic each event was. Being assaulted, being held against my will, feeling trapped in my home with no way out, seeing my sister's dead body so brutally assaulted, being forced to look at her body in the casket, having a knife held between my breasts and feeling the tip go in, being beaten with fists by my husband, these were the ones that stand out the most. During the assessment I remember asking my therapist if seeing my sister's dead body qualified as seeing a "dead body" and her reply was a gentle "yes, Colleen."

I left that session drained, numb and feeling shocked — I had used my pencil to tick off many traumatic events and seeing them accumulated on paper somehow made them all very real and very painful. Grief and sadness remained with me for a few days. I kept going over the test, the events, and how much I had minimized them as "past abuse." Things started to make sense and I could finally say I knew what was going on with my mental health. For months, even years, I had struggled with labels. Other people had said I was irresponsible and dysfunctional, and I even had someone recommend that I seek help for sex addiction. After the assessment was completed and results were given, my official diagnosis was Complex PTSD, which was explained as having severe traumatic events that started as a child, when I faced physical, emotional and sexual trauma with no escape. Later on in my adult life I was in violent, abusive relationships and experienced the traumatic death of my sister Gina. My symptoms included hyper-vigilance, an exaggerated startle reflex, being easily overwhelmed, chronic insomnia, inward and outward rage when things got out of my control, trouble with interpersonal relationships and avoiding close friendships for fear of confrontation, rejection or accountability. I came to understand that PTSD and C-PTSD were very different, with PTSD usually being a reaction to a single event and C-PTSD being defined as multiple or ongoing traumas with the feelings of being trapped that can last from childhood into adulthood. This diagnosis, although devastating, also gave me better insight into what was happening to me, how I could work with my therapist and also how I could minimize the triggers.

Over and over, my experiences with non-Indigenous doctors and nurses were validated as racist, rude or indifferent to my needs. In some instances I would have to educate these poor settlers about the history of colonization in Canada. Most health service providers have no idea about colonization and how it has devastated Indigenous peoples' lives. They are sympathetic when hearing about the horrors of residential schools but it is as if those survivors are still children and not traumatized adults. To them the past is the past, whether it happened 500 years ago or less than fifty years ago. None had heard of the 60s Scoop and it became complicated when I had to do an intake with doctors to discuss my many health issues. I had been diagnosed with insomnia, anxiety and clinical depression in the past, along with high blood pressure, so I required sleeping pills or else I would lie awake all night in bed, my muscles taut with stress, anxiety and worry. If I didn't get enough sleep, I couldn't cope with anything the next day and would spiral into rage, crying or both.

I had done a lot of healing and learning up until this point, but one fall afternoon my son Cree and I were walking in downtown Ottawa when we saw large placards of Indigenous women who had been murdered or gone missing displayed on the steps leading up to the Parliament buildings. On one of the placards was a photo of my late sister-in-law, Lynn. Seeing her face made us sad but we were touched that someone had not forgotten about her unsolved murder. We approached the people holding the vigil and met Bridget Tolley and Kristen Gilchrist-Salles. Bridget was an older woman in her early fifties, quite tall, at least 5'11" with a slim build and curly, shoulder-length hair. She hugged me and told me she was so happy to meet me and to find other family members. We agreed to meet for coffee at a later date. Little did I realize how important these two women would become in my life.

When Bridget and I met a few days later we exchanged stories of our murdered loved ones. Bridget's mother had been struck and killed by a police officer on the Kitigan Zibi reservation in Quebec in October 2001. She created the Families of Sisters in Spirit grassroots organization for families of murdered and missing women when the federal government de-funded the national Sisters in Spirit group. Just because the government decides to de-fund something doesn't mean it's over! Bridget's tenacity and spirited demand for accountability from the Sûreté du Québec (Quebec Police) in the death of her mother had grown into a national role. She now advocates for justice for all families of murdered and missing women especially those murdered by the state, specifically the police state.

Kristen is a settler and ally to Families of Sisters in Spirit. Her role is rooted in supporting Bridget in many ways, like accessing spaces most Indigenous people couldn't or wouldn't access due to lack of resources, racism and educational barriers. I had many long conversations with Kristen, with her listening and helping to make the academic language accessible. Things began to make sense when I applied what I was learning to my accumulated experiences, forever changing my limited view of the world. Kristen was much younger than me and had a youthful energy to her. In some ways she intimidated me but she also fascinated me with all her knowledge of worldly matters. With her dark auburn hair set against her fair skin and fashionable but frugal wardrobe, she was a beauty. As we got to know each other better, I trusted her enough to share some personal stories and in return she just listened, no judgement, no advice — just validation. I had never experienced someone just listening without passing off their own interpretation or opinion of my experiences.

Kristen introduced me to other activists such as the rad Indigenous youth at Native Youth Sexual Health Network, whose work was centered around reproductive justice and sexual health but also deeply centered in supporting bi, queer, trans, disabled women of colour and youth while working towards changing the dialogue of shame, blame and stereotypes attached to body and sexuality. Anti-oppression language was also new in the community. I was being introduced to activists from all walks of life. Some were settlers themselves who identified as "settlers with white privilege" and knew their role was to support and not take over or take up space. "Indigenous solidarity," "anti-oppression work," "prison solidarity," "supporting new settlers," "sex workers" and "harm reduction" were new terms and worldviews that I had not seen or heard at any time before. The language and dialogue that I had been using to talk about people who use drugs, work in the sex trade, have immigrated or have been in prison were extremely ignorant, racist and abusive — and left me feeling shameful. I came to understand that these racist, limited views I had replicated were mainstream and part of colonial Canadian culture. I saw that Canadians loved to hate on folks who were not white, anglophone, able-bodied, straight or fit into their idea of what being "Canadian" meant and this meant you were ostracized, ridiculed, targeted for violent racist rants or even worse, physically assaulted in public. Terms like colonialism, imperialism, capitalism, ableism and sexism helped me understand what exactly was happening and more importantly, understand the issues. I had a choice to either do better or be a willfully ignorant sheep.

It is hard work to continually unlearn and challenge yourself, *honestly* examine your world views, change and do better. You make mistakes, you lose friends and you even have to challenge family members. It makes you uncomfortable, it makes other folks uncomfortable and it may be met with resistance. Family and people you thought were friends will label you a troublemaker. They will say things like "you think you're better than us" and sooner or later you will either drift apart or be forced to make the decision to divorce yourself from these toxic relationships. You will feel guilty at first. I did but I also recognized how toxic and harmful those relationships were to my authentic self. I could not be the person I was meant to be if I remained attached to people who were detrimental to my mental health and well-being.

After recovering from the serious psoriasis flare-up, I was able to get some footage for a documentary I was working on called *The Sixties Scoop: A Hidden Generation*. A friend helped with filming the trailer and we decided to screen it in August 2013. The screening went well but I had to put the documentary on the back burner because I had more health issues. My body ached continuously and my mobility was starting to be affected; I couldn't walk far without complaining of pain, and even walking to the bus stop caused the insides of my legs to burn in protest. Climbing stairs, cleaning the house, taking the laundry to the basement and back upstairs was becoming increasingly difficult. I used to be able to do so much; less than three years prior I had been able to run up three flights of stairs without any pain! I didn't understand what was happening and figured it was because I was getting older. Arthritis and even psoriatic arthritis were disorders I began to research. A referral was sent to a rheumatologist as I waited to find out why my body hurt so much every day.

The rheumatologist looked exactly like Harrison Ford. He asked me a series of questions and then got me to stand up in front of him. He put his fingers on different areas of my body, which caused me immediate and intense pain and brought on tears of protest. "Please stop!" I cried. It felt like he had touched me with a red-hot poker. He touched the eighteen trigger point markers, all the size of pennies, which cause intense pain when pressure is applied. I was given a diagnosis of fibromyalgia, a chronic pain disorder that has no cure and can only be managed with medication, diet and moderate exercise. A diagnosis with no cure left me feeling depressed. Did this mean I would be limited for the rest of my life? Already I had begun to apply for a transfer to a different unit with my housing company.

When a bad fibromyalgia flare-up came, I was forced to stay in bed for days and to use my energy only to cook or shower. My kids had to help me with everything from lifting groceries to doing laundry. They even had to fold it because my arms hurt too much. It was awful and scary to be dependent on others for necessary, everyday activities. Even standing up on the bus was hard: my feet would hurt but even worse, my balance was off and I would become exhausted trying not to fall all over when the bus turned or stopped abruptly. It was a steep learning curve to manage my energy, to make sure I got enough sleep and to limit my activities so that I could carry out necessary activities like grocery shopping or going on outings with friends. I couldn't do the activist work I used to do because it required standing or walking for hours at Parliament Hill or going to late meetings at the last minute. My social life went from super busy to nothing and the pain made me into an exhausted hermit. Learning to manage fibromyalgia symptoms also led me to read that it is connected to PTSD, and in my case, C-PTSD. I understood that being in a state of hyper-vigilance for so long had worn my immune system right down. My body was exhausted and was betraying me.

Another issue that drove me to see a doctor came up because my children, who were older and heading into their twenties, had the courage to tell me that when I raged, I was scary to them. They never knew what would set me off; usually it was some kind of action that would cause me to react violently. The whole house would be upset, with my kids retreating to their bedrooms until I calmed down. Cree and Jonathan would be the catalysts and also the peacemakers, and things would eventually blow over. But a serious incident with one of my son's friends, someone who verbally attacked me in my house and who was being disrespectful, caused me to seek help. The rage I felt at being verbally attacked by someone I had told to leave my house was so intense that I felt I might harm the person. I felt like my blood was boiling and my mind went into overdrive. An overwhelming, uncontrollable feeling of physical strength coursed through my body. I remember grabbing a knife and wanting to harm this person. It reminded me of seeing the Hulk turn green from rage when he was out of control and how scary he was. Did I look like that?

I sought help the next day at the local Indigenous health clinic. Honestly, I was terrified to tell the doctor how I felt for fear he would call the cops or have me arrested for being a danger to the community as a raging Indigenous woman. It was my first time going to the Wabano Health Clinic to see a doctor. In the past I had felt the doctors who worked in other Indigenous clinics were condescending or indifferent. I anxiously waited in the little room and in walked Dr. Bond. This was the first doctor who sat down and really listened to me. He knew about the 60s Scoop adoptions, he understood intergenerational trauma, and when I spoke about rage he understood that also. The best thing Dr. Bond said as he sat across from me was, "As a settler my job is not to make things harder for you. I am here to help you and make accessing health services easier. How can I help you?" When I told him what I needed he said, "I will advocate for you and make sure you get everything you need because you've been through enough already." This blew my mind as no one had ever said that to me except my friend Kristen. Sadly, a month after I initially saw him, he left the clinic to pursue a job up North, but he left referrals and made sure I had follow-up care to pursue the Ontario Disability Support Program.

I had reached a point in my life where I had to stop working because of the chronic pain and constant triggers I experienced on the job. Sitting for long periods was painful, as was standing for longer than five minutes. My mobility had been reduced so much that I couldn't carry the laundry basket and take the stairs at the same time. I also had to make sure I planned outings that didn't require me to stand for too long or walk too far. Sometimes I would be too exhausted and would save my energy for other days when I had important doctor appointments or events. My friends and kids helped me a lot with rides to the grocery store, cleaning my house and doing laundry. This disorder had forced me to manage and conserve my energy and it required me to sacrifice many things I enjoyed — dancing at round dances and inter-tribal pow wows — and it hurt my heart to sit down and watch others dance to the drums.

I decided to focus on my health, to write and to volunteer in my spare time. There was more than enough volunteer work to keep me busy and productive while I focused on self care. Some of the volunteer work I do is with Families of Sisters in Spirit and is rooted in raising awareness about the historical violence women in my own family and others experienced because of forced colonial policies. These policies were meant to erase our identity as Indigenous people by forbidding our language, songs and ceremonies in the making of Canada. Public speaking became vital to my healing. When I first started speaking in public, I couldn't even get through the first few lines without crying or needing a lot of support. But each time I spoke, I got stronger and better at expressing myself and incorporating the many intersectionalities I had learned about.

Word had gone out in the community that I was a dynamic public speaker who talked about missing and murdered Indigenous women and the 60s Scoop. Two of the topics I spoke about and was passionate about were the ways mainstream media perpetuates the myth of Indigenous women as "at risk or deserving of violence," and victim blaming, which ultimately dehumanizes Indigenous women. Connecting violent colonial policies to the making of Canada in the treaty process is the key to understanding why Indigenous people are dehumanized and why Indigenous women continue to be murdered and go missing in Canada. I was careful of who I considered an ally. Not every potential ally has good intentions and some actually perpetuate harm against Indigenous women by refusing to examine their own beliefs and how they might contribute to stereotypes about Indigenous women. I began to be critical of the national Indigenous organizations' agendas; I decided that I would only lend my voice to speak for organizations that were making space for the voices of women with lived experience. I was critical of "white saviors" for trying to "save" sex workers rather than supporting their demands for safer working conditions. Body autonomy became important to me. This stance made enemies of those who perpetuate harm by shaming Indigenous women who choose sex work to get what they need; not just drugs or alcohol but money for tuition, makeup, clothes or whatever they required. My motto was "if it's her body, she decides what she does with it without being assaulted, criminalized or murdered." The harm came from the idea that sex workers are not human or valued. Where does that idea come from? I think it comes from people who perpetuate stereotypes, who believe women are supposed to act a certain way and dress a certain way, and those who don't conform are garbage and asking for violence to happen to them. We have Indigenous women's organizations that say that selling sex is not traditional. In fact our people traded sex for many things — fur, beads, supplies, survival — with settlers and with other Nations. Supporting sex workers became a cause dear to my heart because I had many relatives who chose sex work to survive in Edmonton where racism, poverty and homelessness are prominent thanks to the Canadian government. Violence came with the Europeans and was created in the making of Canada.

Grassroots organizing was at the heart of the work that drew me in. In 2014 a group of local Ottawa adoptees and I decided to host a gathering for Indigenous adoptees of the 60s Scoop. Elaine Kicknosway was one of the 60s Scoop survivors from Saskatchewan who had grown up in Ottawa. Duane Morrisseau Beck was a Métis adoptee living in Ottawa. They stood out as the most devoted and involved when it came to organizing, and they took on the work required to see the gatherings from beginning to end. We all complemented each other and brought different skills to the table. Duane is an outgoing character and I could tell that right away, even though our first interaction was through email. He had heard of our first gathering and registered but began asking a ton of questions about who we were. We met the next day after a flurry of emails back and forth, and immediately hit it off. I admit I was suspicious of him at first and it took time to build trust with him and others. I think he would agree that it also took time for him to trust me. We both had strong personalities and were used to doing things a certain way. Duane has a diplomatic manner and mostly approached this work from a bureaucratic perspective, which represented everything that I resented, so we clashed in some ways when it came to deciding how to proceed as an entity. He was funny at times and sensitive. Sometimes he would cry at the most unexpected times and feel things so deeply. I grew to love him and his partner Craig as family. Even when we had conflict we dealt with it straight on and tried to make sure our working relationship was paramount because the work we were doing was so important to us.

Elaine and I had been friends longer, yet it took a while to develop our friendship and to gain each other's trust. Elaine had a way of keeping people at arm's length because of the work she did but also because trust and vulnerability were issues for her. She didn't let too many people close to her and her family. She was a bit older than me and was well respected in the community as a person who carries ceremonies, conducts sweat lodges and does teachings. She is also a staunch opponent of the Children's Aid Society and advocates for Indigenous children and their families to make sure they are being represented properly. She always wears beautiful handmade ribbon skirts and intricately beaded earrings, and she adorns her very black hair with matching hairpieces. She has a strikingly graceful way about her that makes you feel safe unless you are on her bad side. Then she outright keeps her distance from you, as if your toxic energy will infect her. Trust me, there were more than a few times that she steered clear of people who were either intimidated by her or who she recognized as "popcorn Elders" or fakes. If you go for a ride in Elaine's car, she has a tiny little shell with sage ready to smudge at any moment. This helps her cope with her day-to-day work dealing with child welfare officials. Smudging helped ground us when we were working together and sometimes we would just light it on short road trips to help us in our travels.

Our goal for the 60s Scoop gatherings was to come together, validate and listen to each other's stories and see what transpired from there. For the first gathering we had no funds so we had to raise the money ourselves. I believed we could and we did. The community stepped up to help with in-kind donations and letter-writing campaigns to unions, and we even hosted a karaoke fundraiser with a raffle table. All we needed were funds to pay for the venue, the food and honorariums for Elders, helpers and speakers. We had no funds to help bring adoptees to the gathering but 106 applied and in the end sixty-five attended, with most citing lack of funds as an obstacle to travel. Adoptees and those who experienced foster care as part of the 60s Scoop came from all directions of Turtle Island. We made sure we asked an Algonquin Elder to come give her blessing and acknowledge the territory we were guests on. It came together with barely any effort, like it was meant to happen. The night before the gathering, we were so nervous and tried to cover every possible scenario to avoid any crisis situations, and we asked ourselves, "What have we gotten ourselves into?" Taking lessons from the larger activist community about making safer spaces, inclusivity and utilizing anti-oppressive spaces was a challenge because most of the adoptees doing the organizing had never heard these words before, let alone seen what they look like in action. I wanted to ensure that we used safe approaches and included LGBTQ and folks with disabilities in our organizing.

Excitement was in the air but fear that no one would show up also tugged at my conscience. The morning of our first gathering, we got to the venue early, a sacred fire was lit and the volunteer cooks started putting food out. Slowly the survivors started to trickle in, one by one. They were nervous and apprehensive and we did our best to make sure they felt welcome.

As soon as it started it was over! The whole thing went by in a blur and we applauded ourselves for pulling it off. Most of the feedback was very positive but there were a few complaints, which we took seriously and made sure to learn from. It was a historic and successful 60s Scoop survivor gathering and the beginning of a cross-Canada movement. There were a few of us who wanted to continue doing this work but also take it to the national level. Duane and Elaine became my closest confidantes and colleagues; we were committed to seeing the work through — it was all volunteer work, all done on our own time. There was no other group in Canada doing the kind of work we were doing in Ottawa. We were literally spearheading this movement to create spaces for 60s Scoop survivors' healing, wellness and relearning of our culture. This gave me purpose and got me out of bed every day to continue to build momentum, and to raise funds, share our stories, build community, educate Canadians and international folks about what the Canadian government did to us, and advocate for healing, accountability and funding to continue this work.

There are people who have been on this journey with us and who have continued to support the work we are doing. Fellow 60s Scoop survivor/adoptee Dr. Raven Sinclair was one of the workshop's facilitators who attended each one of our gatherings. She has been instrumental in leading the way as an adoptee and scholar. It was her online article, "Identity Lost and Found: Lessons from the Sixties Scoop," that gave me insight into what happened to my sisters and me.

We were able to secure the involvement of Dennis Windego, an Indigenous therapist specializing in trauma, PTSD and abuse. We also called on Algonquin Elder Albert Dumont and Cree Elders Thomas Loutitt and Irene Lindsay along with guest speaker Conrad Prince, an Ojibway adoptee who had also attended the first national gathering in Alberta in 2007. We had no experience with planning a gathering but we knew we had to have a protocol in place to keep us safe without causing harm to others. Adoptees were on their own unique journeys of healing and we had to recognize that trauma and violence manifest themselves in many ways. We were cautious about inviting non-Indigenous persons into our space because we needed to speak freely without having to worry about hurting non-Indigenous family members' feelings. Monitoring by the government was also a concern but to a much lesser extent since it is no longer illegal for Indigenous people to gather in one place. We figured if they needed to know so badly what we were talking about, they needed to hear the truth. Weeks before the gathering we participated in a sweat lodge to help us do the work and to keep us safe emotionally, spiritually and physically. Every detail was thought out, with care and consideration for each adoptee and foster care survivor who would be coming for the two-day gathering. We realized we might not please everyone who came but we were committed to learning from the experience and doing better at future gatherings.

After the first gathering in September 2014, it took some time to debrief with each other and create a final report. We were astounded that we were able to pull it off with relatively little difficulty and had proven that it was not only meant to be, but that the Creator and our spirit guides were there to help us along the way. In late August 2015, we held our 2nd National 60s Scoop Survivors gathering — at a local campground so we could do sweat lodge and cultural teachings on the land. The gathering included family members of adoptees and those who had experienced foster care. The gathering had fewer people this time but the smaller group made it more intimate and manageable. We did workshops surrounding the sacred fire, made drums, offered art therapy and roasted marshmallows under the stars. At times it felt like we were kids all over again on a camping sleepover. The gatherings gave us new memories of acceptance, the feeling that we fit in somewhere, and a sense of family support.

~~~

We have kept in touch over the years and remain supportive in all our joys, successes and hard times. The National Indigenous Survivors of Child Welfare Network has grown considerably, with more and more survivors reaching out to us for support, validation, information and resources. I continue to do public presentations about the 60s Scoop and am regularly invited to university and college classes, community organizations and spaces across Turtle Island. I speak to people who want to learn about how colonial child welfare policies have impacted and interrupted Indigenous peoples' lives, and about the work that needs to be done to make it right, to help us heal and to never allow it to happen again.

In September 2015 I was able to return to my community of Onihcikiskowapowin (Saddle Lake Cree Nation, Alberta) to record footage for my documentary, *The 60s Scoop: A Hidden Generation.* I had secured a grant that helped pay for equipment, travel and expenses. My intent was to try to interview my birth family, to capture their stories, and to ask to use them in my film. The trip had a dual purpose: I was also there to give a presentation on Indigenous women and their families to the Edmonton Police Victim Services Conference for Missing and Murdered Persons.

My son Cree accompanied me to our territory. He had not been back to Alberta since we left when he was five years old. This was a big adventure for him to return, to visit relatives he had never met and to capture some video footage. Cree took a Greyhound bus, a gruelling two-night trip, by himself. This was the first time he had travelled alone. Returning to Edmonton filled me with anxiety. I worried that I would be triggered by memories of violence and my sister's murder. There were many thoughts that swirled inside my head so I needed to put tobacco down, let things happen as they would and keep my spirit safe.

This was the first significant amount of time Cree and I had ever spent together, just the two of us. We had been through some rough patches since his teenage years and lately we had been at each other's throats. He resented me for many years for leaving his father and we had some differences we needed to resolve, but we put those issues on the back burner to make this trip together. I felt that he needed to go back "home" to heal, and also that seeing where he came from would help him understand the choices I had made.

Cree has always been headstrong, opinionated and the protector in our family. In some ways he has had to be the man and raise his little brother, too. Our first night in Edmonton was spent meeting his cousins on his dad's side; it was wonderful for him to see faces like his own. People marvel at how much he looks like his dad.

The presentation for the Edmonton Victim Services was a huge success and the biggest venue I've spoken at to date. The room was filled with police officers, social workers and frontline workers, first responders when people are murdered or go missing. Public speaking has become a passion of mine; at one time speaking to groups of people would have caused me to have heart palpitations, break out in a sweat and want to vomit. Now I get a high from public speaking that lasts for hours, but then my body crashes and needs rest. One aspect that makes my presentations so compelling is the connection of broader issues to my own personal narrative.

The day after my presentation, Cree and I left our hotel and took the LRT to downtown Edmonton. My goal was for us to visit the park where my sister had been killed. Cree was my rock. We brought along a camera to film some footage for the documentary I was working on. There had been many changes since the last time I had been to that park. New buildings, landscaping, foliage and sculptures gave the park a different feel. I wasn't sad or overcome with grief this time; I felt calm and at peace. The park was situated on a busy corner in downtown Edmonton and there was a lot of foot traffic during the day. Twenty years prior, small hills had provided the perfect cover for drug deals, assaults and even some sex work. Now the hills had been flattened and we could see right through the park, so the chances of criminal activity taking place there were diminished. I never thought the day would come that I could remember my beloved older sister, who had died so violently and alone in this park, without suffering intense pain. But my heart had healed and my eyes didn't fill with tears this time. I smiled and put some tobacco down on the grass, prayer offerings for Gina's grown children who were now struggling with drug and alcohol addiction themselves. The legacy of Canada's colonial child welfare policies is still reverberating through our own children; they inherited our trauma.

After we visited the park, we got on the highway and travelled to Onihcikiskowapowin (Saddle Lake Cree Nation) with some friends who had offered to let us stay with their relatives on the reserve. These people were strangers to us but they opened up their homes and hearts to allow us to feel safe and accepted while we did the important work of reconnecting to our community. On the two-hour trip along the highway to Saddle Lake, the land brought calmness and peace to my heart. It was familiar. We passed buffalo grazing beside the highway and the driver pulled over so I could admire them and take photos. Seeing those buffalo was overwhelming. Tears were on the edges of my eyelids and gratitude is the only way I could explain this moment.

Our host had prepared a huge dinner to welcome us to her house and to Saddle Lake. It was almost 10 p.m. and Cree and I were exhausted. When we went out to the van to get our luggage, we couldn't help but look up and revel at the trillions of stars that lit up the sky and how quiet the night was. You could see the universe! We slept like babies that night and were up at the crack of dawn with our host for breakfast. She let us use her van for the duration of our stay and explained how to get around Saddle Lake. I would have gotten lost easily without her carefully drawn directions! After breakfast I ventured outside to take a look around; we had ridden in complete darkness the previous night so I was curious to see the land. The unobstructed flatness of the land caused me to stretch my arms on either side of my body and gaze in each direction. I noted how my arms were parallel with the ground as my fingertips touched the horizons on each side. It was sublime. I wonder if my ancestors also marvelled at the vast expanse of the land.

EverythingIknewaboutgettingaroundOnihcikiskowapowin community revolved around a gas station called Bison Auto Stop, which was where everyone went to check their mail and gas up. I had these little scraps of paper with roughly drawn maps of where my relatives lived and how to get to them, complete with little squares representing houses and band offices. These little drawings are tucked away forever with my keepsake items as a reminder of my time in my community. The thing I noticed right away was that people stared at my son and me because they didn't know who we were. The second thing was that everyone shook hands and greeted each other kindly, with affection and respect. We never did that in the city! And the third thing was they always asked right away who your parents or your *kokum* were. People were very friendly and my heart soared.

I had not experienced this my first time in Onihcikiskowapowin when I was sixteen years old and had gone there to meet my *kokum* and other family members. There was no real welcome from the community on that occasion, no acknowledgement of what had happened, nor were there any stories, warm greetings or smiles. It was a sad, bittersweet time. Going back at the age of forty-three was very different. People were very warm and treated me as if they knew me, although once again there was no acknowledgement from the Chief and council that I had been taken from them. I would have liked a ceremony to welcome me back, to say they missed me, that I was wanted and valued. I think that feeling resonates among 60s Scoop adoptees. We are still waiting for our welcoming ceremonies.

Cree and I made our way to Blue Quills College, a former residential school that my mother had attended from 1962 to 1966. Blue Quills has been at the current location since 1931 and it became the first Indigenous controlled school in 1971 when twelve surrounding First Nations communities staged a sit-in at the school to demand control of the facility and assume responsibility for their own children's education. It was a truly historical and successful initiative that is thriving to this day. Blue Quills was close to becoming an accredited university. Driving up the gravel road to the familiar red brick building brought on a mix of emotions, both uneasiness and trepidation at the unknown. The leaves on the windy gravel driveway had already turned red, orange and yellow and they swirled around the car while hundreds of snow geese flew overhead. Those snow geese would be food for our northern brothers and sisters!

Cree and I walked into the building and explored on our own. We visited the library archives, scouring the yearbooks for any photos of my mother but there was only a single photo of her. I scanned the black and white photos of these children looking for familiar features and trying to interpret the expressions of the students — anything to give me an indication of happiness, sadness, desperation or resentment. This skill I had developed in childhood of detecting emotions through hyper-vigilance didn't work too well for photographs, but I tried.

Cree and I then decided to explore the grounds outside the school. We cautiously headed down a small dirt road around the back of the school that allowed for only one vehicle to pass. Admittedly the fear of bears made me hesitate but Cree assured me we would be safe. Colourful prayer flags hung in the trees, which caused us to turn off our cameras to respect those prayers and then all of a sudden, tucked away behind the trees in a large opening, we saw eight or nine massive teepee frames and four sweat lodge frames looking like skeletons on the land. Immediately I felt a strong desire in my heart to spend time in this space. Later I would learn that Blue Quills hosts a big culture camp in the spring on the land where ceremony and teachings are shared. It is my goal to return to my homelands and learn those ceremonies.

My paternal Aunty Silver caught up with us at the Blue Quills. She had attended the residential school as a little girl and offered to give us a tour. Before we entered the building, she talked about a young boy who jumped out of the window to his death and the somber mood was set. That story stayed with me throughout the day. What horrors that boy must have lived with that death was better than living in that residential school. While Aunty Silver told this story, Cree was up on the fire escape filming and could not hear her speaking. She did not want to be filmed or recorded, she just wanted to share and leave it alone so I respected her wishes. This tour would be hard on her but she was adamant to show us around the school. We started in the basement where the kids would take their meals. She explained how the girls and boys were separated and not allowed to talk even if they were siblings. Aunty Silver pointed to different places, small rooms or nondescript cubbyholes where she remembered bad things had happened to students. She was visibly shaken by those memories and the stories she had heard. As we ventured up the stairs, I put my hand on the railing and instantly was jolted with images of the hundreds of other little hands that had touched the railing, of the hundreds of children who had ventured upstairs over the years they spent captive in that school. My soul physically felt this image and I wonder if one of those little hands was my mother's, aunties' or uncles' who attended this school back in the day.

Aunty Silver showed us the dorm rooms and where the nuns used to sleep. She shared stories of the girls she went to school with but there were certain rooms she would not go into and to tell you the truth, I didn't like the feelings in those rooms either. Aunty Silver invited us to visit her at the Elders' complex later, so we hugged and I thanked her for sharing with us, as difficult as it was, and we went our separate ways.

My time in my community was short but memorable and mostly positive, so much so that I long to return and attend University nuhelot'įne thaiyots'į nistameyimâkanak Blue Quills to learn my language and also to teach it. The reality is that it would be next to impossible for me to move from Ontario to Alberta. I could not uproot my children again and besides, none of my children want to return to Edmonton. Their home is in Ottawa now.

I visited my paternal Aunty Dee who was overjoyed to see me and to meet Cree. She had many stories to share with me of my dad, my mom, my *kokum* and how she remembered when we were taken away. Aunty Dee also did not wish to be recorded and I respected her wishes. It was very hard for my family to share their pain and memories. She shed many tears as she recalled how her mother — my *kokum* — was devastated to lose us as babies. Hearing these memories from her caused my heart to feel whole because up until this point I had believed no one even cared about us as children, no one talked about us or missed us. This told me that, yes, my sisters and I were missed and our *kokum* loved us. My dad, however, had always discouraged me from going back to my community and talking to people. He said he did not want me stirring things up and asked me to leave it alone. *But how could I leave this alone?*

One of the last places I visited before I left Onihcikiskowapowin was my birth mother's gravesite. Dolly Esther died in 1999 and I had not grieved her passing. At that time my heart felt nothing for a woman I barely knew. No one told me before she died that she had attended residential school, nor had they shared any stories of her. It was through my own research in 2013 that I discovered she had been at Blue Quills for four years. This news changed my view of her. For the longest time I held resentment towards her. I remembered her being drunk the first time I met her in Edmonton and the feelings of shame, disgust and anger that my body held onto for many years, even at my sister's funeral. I wanted to lash out at her, blame her for my sister's death, for her drunkenness.

In one moment of clarity and sympathy, I realized the pain, shame, guilt and grief that my late mother must have felt when we were taken, too much for one person to endure. Regardless of her choices, the empathy and understanding that grew in my heart for her caused me to recognize how immature, selfish and angry I had been. How could I have known?

Shannon Houle, an Onihcikiskowapowin band councillor, helped me find my birth mother's death certificate at the church on the Onihcikiskowapowin reserve, then we headed over to her gravesite. It was an enormous site and I worried it would take all day to find her grave. Shannon went off to look for her own relatives while I searched for mine. My camera was filming as I wandered through the rows and rows of wooden crosses. Some of the graves had fancy stones but not too many. At one point I said out loud, "Where are you, Mom?" and I took five steps and looked down. Her cross was broken in two in the ground in front of me and the words "Dolly Cardinal 1950–1999" were written on it. Just like that, her cross kind of fell into my path. Out of the thousands of grave markers we could not believe how easily we had found it. My late maternal Aunties Roseanne, Cece and Albertine and my Uncle Marvin were all buried alongside her. Shannon covered me with a shawl, gave me a pouch of tobacco and left me alone with my thoughts and words for my late mom. Acknowledging my mom as my lifegiver and someone who suffered and drank herself to her grave, I forgave her and myself for all the hurtful feelings I had towards her. My heart was full and I did not cry. I felt happy and free, like I had come full circle. I now carry a tattoo of her name on my left forearm so I never forget her in my daily life. I want other survivors to know that you can go home — and you can be angry, and you can forgive, however long it takes.

~~~

In many conversations with my birth father he seemed angry and resentful. I don't blame him, but the amount of internalized racism he carried towards our own people was discouraging and harmful to my spirit. When I lived in Edmonton it was normal to hear racist and homophobic words. I even uttered them myself because I didn't know any better. But I have since learned that these words are inappropriate and can be deeply hurtful. I no longer tolerate racism or homophobia in my life, yet when I tell my birth father that I do not like him using racist words, he continues. It scares me that he has so much hatred toward anyone who is an immigrant or Black. My son Cree was a witness to his *moosum's* violent behaviour in the short time they spent together. My birth father and I are not close and communication is limited to protect my heart.

As hurtful as it may be to say, I feel disconnected from my birth family, even after this return to my homelands. I feel more like a visitor or even an intruder than a valued family member. Being estranged from my adoptive family also left a huge hole in my heart that my children and grandchildren now fill, along with the many adoptee friends who have become my family of choice.

This is the legacy of colonization and colonial child welfare policies — these policies created by non-Indigenous settlers have ripped apart and ruined Indigenous family systems for generations. For many years I romanticized my relationships with my birth and adoptive families, always playing my part as a daughter hoping we would be this happy, supportive, loving family like the white families I saw in television sitcoms. Pining for the love and affection from my adoptive mom and birth father that I never received has worn me down. Not once in my life have these people told me they loved or cared about

me. Not once. I learned what love is and how to love uncondi-
tionally from my children, my grandchildren and the very close
friends who are my family of choice. They give me lots of hugs,
kisses on the cheek, with no expectations. They listen without
telling me what I should do or how I should act. They let me figure things out on my own but are ready to assist if I ask for help.
I can talk about my dreams without being censored or shut
down. I used to fear that I would hurt my white family's feelings or be called "racist" if I brought up colonization, racism or
white privilege. I learned how to be single and happy without
being co-dependent or using sex as a replacement for the love I
never received as a child from my fathers, my brothers, uncles
and partners. Most importantly, I learned to love myself. It's not
perfect by any means and it's still a lot of work having chronic
illnesses like psoriasis, fibromyalgia and C-PTSD, diabetes and
high blood pressure that require daily medications, eating
properly and not overdoing things. I have been a workaholic
since I was a child thanks to the arduous mandatory labour in
my adoptive home and being pushed to excel, work hard and be
the best, often to the detriment of my health, but I find it hard
to change. Sometimes it's a gift and a curse at the same time
because I don't know how to relax when I should. I am grateful
for my ability to understand my trauma, to recover and manage
my symptoms so I can continue doing work that enriches and
helps other survivors. It is truly a blessing.

# CHAPTER 10

# Miiyo-pimaatisoowin

IN RECENT YEARS, I have been able to change my perspective of myself as the victim by examining my experiences over the decades and tracing the colonial violence in my family right back to the making of Canada. I was never meant to find out what happened to my family, let alone find my parents, endure the violence, heal from the trauma and put the pieces together about how the state intended to assimilate me into the mindless tax-paying Canadian citizenry. The state has never been invested in making sure I retained my culture, land base or knowledge, nor was it concerned that my health and well-being as a First Nations ward of the Crown was protected. This would lead me to believe that everything I had learned up to this point about the state in its dealings with First Nations people was deliberate in its intent to erase us from the history of this country.

The trauma and loss I experienced compelled me to write my story and speak out about the abuses I endured. The shame I felt might have silenced me forever so I am grateful for the helpers who came into my life and encouraged me to change that shame into courage. As painful as it was, it also set me on a healing journey that has lasted a lifetime and is still going. There is no more protection for my abusers and I have left it in the Creator's hands. My late sister Gina has been with me in spirit this whole time and my sister Dakota is on my mind daily. Gina didn't get to finish her journey and Dakota is still on hers and I pray for her every day that she finds her voice and makes peace with that part of her childhood that changed our lives forever. She may never make the connection but I did and that is something I can pass on for generations through storytelling in my family. I realized at one point there would be no one left to tell the story if I didn't tell it. How would my sister's children in foster care come to know who their mother really was and what she went through as a child? I am grateful after all these years that they are in my life because for so long I thought they were lost to the child welfare system. They ask me questions about their mom and what she was like and I remind them that she loved them and tried to be a good mom. I tell them stories of her as a child and how much she loved to draw, and how her trauma and abuse led to her addiction. Maybe Gina's great-grandchildren will eventually want to research and find out about their great-grandmother. Who knows, but it will be in writing for them if they seek it out. It's all there in the story of how the women in my family have been impacted due to forced colonial policies that are still rippling through our family to this day. My only hope is that the next generation will be able to turn it around and not repeat it or let it happen again. I do not want my grandchildren and great-grandchildren to inherit the damaging effects of systemic racism, to feel ashamed to be Indigenous. I want them to continue to fight against injustice, to change the narrative and be proud to be Indigenous.

I've been called a troublemaker, angry, stuck in the past and even radical because I choose to give voice to my pain and my healing. I've even been threatened with legal action for speaking the truth. I have only spoken from my lived experiences and those things I have been witness to — nothing more, nothing less. Despite the chronic pain from fibromyalgia that invades my body daily and cripples me sometimes, and the immense task of managing C-PTSD symptoms, the Creator has helped me craft my experiences into something worth sharing, something to help others learn and heal also. I consider myself very fortunate to be able to tell my story and have the insight because so many are still on their journeys, and there are more to come. We need to tell our stories, have our stories validated and create a movement through healing, understanding and supporting each other.

Don't get me wrong: I am far from 100 percent healed. Sometimes "Thank You" by Led Zeppelin makes me sob, but mostly I smile. It depends on my mood. Certain things will trigger me, like pictures of my sisters and me as young girls, and certain smells remind me of Island Lake where we grew up. Even this writing hurts sometimes. My chest will feel heavy, my body will ache, and that will make me stop everything for a few days until I am ready to tackle it again.

The people I have needed the most in my life came in the form of other 60s Scoop survivors, community activists, non-Indigenous allies, academics, grassroots organizers, my children and grandchildren. My goal is to surround my children, my grandchildren and myself with reciprocal love, safety, tenderness, kindness and unconditional love regardless of identity, gender or race. Each day I reach my goal, and it feels good.

As we do this work together, united in our cause to remedy the injustices committed against us, the common bond connecting us is rooted in living well, keeping each other safe, treating each other gently and with love, and recognizing our uniqueness and common struggles. We are supporting and lifting each other up so we can all move forward together.

*Ekosi pitama*

# Epilogue

ONE THING THAT I could not have predicted when I started this journey was the number of 60s Scoop survivors who would come into my life. I have personally met over 400 survivors of the 60s Scoop at the gatherings and I have talked with some on the phone, on Facebook and through email. Each and every survivor I have met has shared their story and brought a sense of hope, healing and community. Adoptees from as far away as Britain and Australia, from the United States, and from all the provinces and territories in Canada have touched my life and shared their stories. I'm so grateful to them and many I consider my family. My hope is that survivors and others who experienced foster care may find peace and healing in whatever form they come.

Just recently, in August 2017, a month before our National Indigenous Survivors of Child Welfare Network 3rd Bi-Giwen National Gathering, I got news from my biological aunt that I should call my dad in Edmonton because my younger brother Richard had passed away. I wasn't very close to my dad anymore or to Richard but I still felt overwhelming grief for my dad's loss of his only son. They were very close and my dad took care of him daily. Richard was younger than me, a very large man who had been diagnosed with diabetes at eighteen and had already had his leg amputated due to his condition. He had been admitted to the hospital for complications and passed in his sleep at the age of forty-two. I couldn't go to the funeral due to lack of funds and my dad said not to bother, but

I grieved quietly and alone for my dad's loss. It was a sobering reminder of how detached and disconnected I really am from my family of birth.

Our Network held its third national gathering from September 27 to October 1, 2017, with seventy-five survivors coming from all over Turtle Island and one from New Zealand. We co-hosted an exhibition dedicated to creating awareness about the 60s Scoop that highlights ten survivors' stories and will travel across Canada. For five days, beginning with the lighting of the sacred fire, we held workshops on Conflict Resolution, Trauma, Healing the Man, Spiritual Abuse, Loss and Grief, Art Therapy and Clan Teachings, drum and rattle making, sweats and LGBTQ teachings, and we even held a Christmas dinner with a giveaway afterwards. Survivors brought items to share, from art to candles, fabric and medicines. The Network was able to give each survivor a T-shirt, a bag with a logo, a plastic bracelet that said, "I'm not the Only One," a pen and a magnet. They were so happy with the unexpected gifts. The survivors socialized throughout the days and evenings, they sat by the fire, hugged, shared, drummed, sang, played board games, laughed a lot and at the end, when it was time to leave, shed lots of tears together. Our hearts, bellies and minds were full of new experiences, teachings, new friends and family to carry us through when we felt alone. The most touching event at this gathering was the blanketing ceremony hosted by my friend and Elder Leroy Bennett, who gave a teaching about the blankets we receive during our lifetime and the significance of those blankets. A lot of survivors have not been welcomed back into their communities yet, so we at the Network decided to blanket and welcome each other home in a ceremony. The blankets were blessed by the Elder, and Duane, Elaine, our new board member Vicky and I blanketed each survivor. It was a very emotional ceremony, with survivors breaking out in tears, overwhelmed at finally being acknowledged and welcomed back into the circle and a community of survivors. At times while I was blanketing survivors, tears welled up in my eyes because I could relate to how they felt and how much it meant to be welcomed and to feel connected to other survivors.

The Network had a special surprise. Months before, we had requested a handmade star blanket to honour Raven Sinclair for all her work, past and present, for 60s Scoop survivors. Receiving a star blanket from your community is one of the highest honours. It means you've done good work and deserve to be acknowledged. Raven's work inspired me and others, her writing created change, pushed social workers to do better in their jobs, and led to policies being enacted that impact Indigenous people's lives. It was sublime to blanket her. She did not expect it but happily accepted it, with tears and hugs all around.

The most amazing moment for me at the end of the gathering was having an Honour song sung for me, for the work I've dedicated my life to and for helping other survivors like myself. We hugged the survivors, sometimes for minutes, with tears in our eyes, promising to keep in touch on Facebook. Later that week we got word that the federal government would be making an announcement to 60s Scoop survivors about a settlement for the Ontario class action lawsuit. This news set us in crisis mode, scrambling to respond to Indian Affairs Minister Carolyn Bennett with a press conference in the Parliament building. We hadn't even had time to debrief from the gathering or catch our breaths before dozens of us from across the country were being asked for interviews by every news station!

The announcement came with the decision that 60s Scoop survivors would receive $25,000 to $50,000 each, depending on how many plaintiffs qualified, but it excluded Métis and non-status Indigenous persons, which was disappointing and created anger amongst survivors across Canada. It caused anxiety for the many people left wondering if they qualified and anger at the small amount of money that would be distributed for the many losses we had experienced. Many survivors were triggered and re-traumatized from having to deal with the decision without warning and without emotional supports in place. There was so much confusion and misinformation being passed around on Facebook and through the media. We were told that, along with the monetary compensation, a healing foundation would be formed with an infusion of $50 million. We have yet to learn how that money will be distributed. It has been a trying time for everyone affected. The Network was inundated with requests for TV appearances and radio interviews where we were asked how we felt about the settlement and the healing foundation funds that were announced. We have a good media communications person who was able to get coverage throughout the US and overseas, with interviews and articles reaching the Canadian Press, Al Jazeera, and the British and European presses. Even Barcelona called for an interview. People in other countries could not understand how Canada could get away with trafficking Indigenous children all over the world. They wanted to know all the details and how we felt about the compensation.

The Network has deliberately remained impartial to the monetary compensation, focusing instead on healing and wellness through culture, advocacy, awareness and building community for 60s Scoop survivors. We had already been slowly but steadily moving toward operationalizing, but increasing numbers of survivors are now calling for action as well as compensation for our losses.

As quickly as interest in 60s Scoop survivors grew and the frenzy of activity happened, they went away and the mainstream media moved on to more pressing issues. Yet survivors are still in the dark, left to navigate their way through all the confusing information about accessing settlement funds, finding adoption and foster care records, applying for Indian Status and dealing with the overwhelming emotions this announcement created.

The announcement did not signal closure or a happy ending. We are not even close to being done. If anything, we are just on the cusp of creating change, healing and making headway with healing initiatives. The announcement was the tip of the iceberg when it comes to the state righting the wrongs of the past. The gatherings have been a good place to start on our agenda, and they have been a huge success, incorporating ceremonies and workshops to help survivors build a toolbox to carry throughout their lives. However, we need dedicated funding to continue doing this work, and the work needs to be led by survivors like myself because we are the ones who know what we need to heal. Survivors are the experts.

~~~

I will leave you with a final thought and a suggestion for fellow survivors. Hold in your heart compassion, empathy and understanding for yourself and for all our adoptee/foster-cared brothers and sisters who are missing and murdered, living with and struggling with addictions, managing mental health and/ or undiagnosed mental health issues, surviving in the sex trade, experiencing homelessness, or living with HIV/AIDS, diabetes or chronic pain. Pray for and participate in action to support our many incarcerated brothers and sisters, and especially our Indigenous youth, who are now so over-represented and under-funded in the child welfare systems across Turtle Island, otherwise known as Canada. Most of all, take care of yourself. You are not alone.

*Kâhiyâw niwâhkomâkanak* — All My Relations

# Glossary

*Ohpikiihaakan-ohpihmeh* [oopik keehah kun-ooh pimeh]
  – brought up somewhere else
*kiskisonaw kahkiiyaw ka-saakihaayaakik*
  – we remember all our loved ones
*Tapeyihtamiwin* – Reckoning
*Nehiiyaw iskwew* – Plains Cree woman
Chapter 1 – *E-maskamih cik* – they take them away from
Chapter 2 – *Tasoosiw* – trapped
Chapter 3 – *Môniy'w* – white men
Chapter 4 – *Tapasiiwin* – running away
Chapter 5 – *Maayipayowin* – adversity
Chapter 6 – *Paspiiwin* – survival
Chapter 7 – *E-tipayimsoowin* – being boss of yourself
Chapter 8 – *Ekaa naantaw kaa-wiikihk* – homelessness
Chapter 9 – *Naahta-wiikewin* – healing
Chapter 10 – *Miiyo-pimaatisoowin* – the good life

# Acknowledgements

TO DR. RAVEN SINCLAIR, who has become a friend, mentor and colleague, and who helped greatly to get this book published.

To Kristen Gilchrist-Salles and Bridget Tolley of Families of Sisters in Spirit for listening, believing in me and never, ever, trying to change me but accepting me the way I am, flaws and all.

To Nisikos Mary Collins Cardinal for helping to get the correct meaning and spelling of the Plains Cree language.

To Rebekka Augustine (MercuryWorks Editing) for your excellent editing skills.

To Margie Kristjansson, first for your friendship but also for your archival research, feedback and editing.

To Duane, Elaine, Lesley, Bev, Dan, Sarah, Elizabeth, Shawn, Shaun, Tealey, Vicki, Nakuset, Nina, Chandra, Dawn and Bob (lol) and the many, many survivors who have touched my life with their incredible spirit, resilience and compassion and who have become my family of choice.

To my estranged childhood friends for your friendship, even though we don't speak any more. You encouraged and supported me on countless occasions. Thank you.

To the adoptees and foster care brothers and sisters, please know that you are not alone. We are all connected by our common experiences and we are here waiting for you.

Lastly, but most importantly, to my children and grandchildren for picking me as your mom and *kokum*. You were my reason for living, my reason to keep going no matter what. You are my everything — my hopes, my dreams, my comfort, my family and my universe.